World War II Memories

Leonard Zerlin

Up Front In World War II, by Bill Mauldin
Reprinted by permission of the author and the Watkins/Loomis Agency, Inc.

The Best From Yank, The Army Weekly
Reprinted by permission of Penguin, U.S.A.

World War II: A Statistical Survey by John Ellis
Reprinted by permission of Facts on File, Inc.

Insignia and Medals
Reprinted by permission of the Department of the Army
Institute of Heraldry

Library of Congress
Catalog Card Number 96-069487

Copyright, Leonard Zerlin 1996 ©
ISBN 0-9653520-0-5

Foreword

World War II...Memories is a book for all veterans.

It includes all the slang and expressions that were a part of our world, from Ack-Ack to Zippo. (No expletives deleted.) In these pages you'll find hundreds of songs, vocalists and bands that were most popular during the war years, Bill Mauldin cartoons of Willie, Joe, Sad Sack, service songs, excerpts from Yank magazine, pictures, letters from G.I.s, poems, statistics; from battle casualties in all theaters of operations to bombing missions, tonnage of bombs dropped, type of aircraft, ships and submarines built, aces of all the belligerent nations, medals and insignia of all branches, and so much more.

For veterans, this book will be a nostalgic trip to the past, and an heirloom for the families to treasure long after we old fogies are gone. It will paint a picture of the life we lived and the world we shared. There are no heroes or feats of daring. It was written for the millions of us that participated in this conflict and wish to remember or share with our loved ones some of the memories.

Table of Contents

Acknowledgements

I wish to thank Nancy Haberman of Desktop Design, and her assistant Sharon Hardee for their dedication and patience in getting this entire effort published. Compiling all the material into a logical format was most difficult and time consuming. Without them, *World War II...Memories* would probably still be in its infant stages.

The professionalism and experience of Bob Arlow, my friend and newspaper columnist, was instrumental in restructuring the book, translating my English into readable form. In Brooklyn, I guess we never did loin to speak da language or dot de eyes...

Youse is a good friend, Bob, and I'll discount your copy.

Support of my veteran friend, ex-Lt. Ted Rosenthal was invaluable, assisting in generating computer savvy to an illiterate novice, and offering slang, songs, advice and counsel.

Letters of encouragement from vets throughout the country gave me the push when I thought this effort was too difficult.

And of course to my entire family for allowing me the freedom to pursue this idea.

Preface

A few months before the 50th anniversary of D-Day, I wrote the following letter to about 20 newspaper editors around the country. A number of newspapers printed the letter or editorialized on it. Many of you read it and wrote me. Some of your letters are reprinted in this book.

Editor;

I got to thinking that this year is the 50th anniversary of VE and VJ day. Time is short so.... Need your help. I am compiling a book of memorabilia on WWII that will list expressions, sayings, songs, and experiences that were part of our service experience.

For those of us that still have our faculties, who are still around, looking down at the roses... before we start looking up at the roses.

Things like;

Gold brick, SNAFU, Kilroy was here, Chicken ——, Short arm, etc. Also some songs like; Roll Me Over in the Clover, or The pancakes that they serve us, they say is very fine, One fell off the table, and killed a friend of mine....

Words or versions of songs...marching songs... verses,. bar room songs...

Barracks humor or any short humorous or harrowing experience relating to those few short years where friendships and comaraderie had meaning.

They can be ribald, raucous, ridiculous, but true. I will not censor four letter words...(There will be no expletives deleted!)

Get your thinking caps on, take your Geritol, and let's think back to a period of our distant past.

Leonard Zerlin
3232 Lanier Pl.
Thousand Oaks, Ca. 91360
(805) 492-2272

Introduction

In terms of a lifetime, the few short years we spent in the service of our country were but a tiny fraction of our human experience. But, in reality, they had an indelible influence upon us by molding values and perceptions that unquestionably shaped the world in which we live.

By today's standard, we are an anachronism, believing in HONOR, INTEGRITY, and RESPONSIBILITY.

From a country at peace, we joined together in unanimity of purpose, and at no time in human history was there a greater resolve to join together, to right the unprovoked dastardly attack upon our nation, and destroy the evils of a maniacal dictatorship.

Overnight, we produced planes and tanks, guns and ammunition, weapons of war at a rate that only a democratic and united country could achieve. Until we learned the horrors and ineptitude of unpreparedness, we suffered severe losses in all theaters of operations, but we survived—and learned quickly. And learn we did! And when it was all over, we graciously forgave our enemies, rebuilt their cities and financed their recovery.

It made young boys into men, cementing indelible bonds of friendship and camaraderie. We shared: the mess hall, the galley, head and latrine, beaches, fox-holes, Quonset huts and barracks, the hard bunks, freezing weather and drafty tents, the mud, snipers, and C rations, missions, pot belly stoves and stories of home. We shared the loss of comrades and grieved, each in our own way. We learned the lessons of war. And we who survived this experience can never forget. We have memories that linger as long as we shall live.

We had our own language and expressions, songs, terminology and stresses in this volatile period. We griped at everything and lived with rumors that either elated or depressed us, but it was part of our universe. Only those of us who lived it can truly appreciate the memory. Our spouses might understand, our children be casually attentive to our stories, our grandchildren look with boredom or shake their heads at the antiquity of this period in history—but WE are the living recipients of this experience.

Yes, we of this geriatric generation made it happen.

So after much thought, I decided to delve into my fading recollections, then enlist the aid of all you veterans to assist in writing this diary; to capture a bit of the nostalgia and memory just a SHORT FIFTY ODD YEARS AGO!

If you like the effort, let me know, or if you can add some more useful information for a future updated edition, please write. But if you don't like the contents...piss off!!!

Slang & Expressions

Blow it out...

Scuttlebutt

Blockbuster

Flub the Dub

Chickenshit

Jungle Juice

Clap Shack

Brown Nose

Milk Run

Sad Sack

Dogface

Dry Run

Got a Dose

SOS

Bomber's Moon

FUBAR

Toyko Rose

Doodle Bugs

Flack Happy

SNAFU

Piss Call

The Eagle Shits Today

Kilroy Was Here

Glossary of World War II
Slang and Expressions
(Rated PG-17)

NOTE: Explanations are given for those whose branch of service didn't reflect those terms of endearment!

Ack-Ack	Anti-Aircraft Fire
Army	A body of men assembled to rectify the mistakes of the diplomats
Any gum, chum?	British youths soliciting Yanks for gum
Axis Sally	Propaganda broadcaster from Germany
Bed Check	Bunk inspection
Bed Check Charlie	Lone enemy plane awakening sleeping troops
Behind the Eight Ball	Screwing Up
Blitz	Bombing of London
Blockbuster	Massive bomb
Blow It Out	Your ass...barracks bag
Bomber's moon	Clear night for bombing
Brown Nose	Gained favors with Sgt. or officer to keep out of detail
Brass	High-ranked officer
BTO	Bombing Through Overcast. Radar equipment made this possible
Bucking for Sec 8	Looking for early discharge
Bunk Fatigue	Excessive free time
Burma Road	Supply route to India
Burp Gun	German semi or automatic weapon
Butt End Charlie	Tail gunner
Butterfly Bomb	Slow descending bomb
C Rations	The least popular packaged G.I. food
C.B.I.	Caribbean, Burma, India, theater of operations
Chicken Colonel	Unnecessary discipline, petty regulations and abused authority
Chickenshit	Degrading term for petty grievance
Chow Mobile	Mobil kitchen
Chow Hound	First in line for chow
Clap Shack	Sick Bay
Colonel Blimp	British cartoon character

Combat Fatigue	Excessive exposure to battle
Desert Fox	Nickname of Field Marshal Rommell
Desert Rats	British Seventh Armored Division. Named by Mussolini
Dirty Girtie of Bizerte	Unprintable song
Dogface	Foot soldier, private
Dog Robber	GI who was butler or valet to officers
Doodle Bugs	Robot bombs
Doughfoot	Foot soldier
Dovetails	WAC 2nd Lt.
Droop Snoop	P-38 modified for photo reconnaissance or precision bombing
Drop your cocks an' grab your socks	Wake-up call
DP	Displaced Persons
Dry Run	Simulated bombing
Dugout Doug	General MacArthur
Eager Beaver	Always anxious to volunteer or please
E.T.O.	European Theater of Operations
Eight Ball, or Behind the eight ball	All screwed up
Feather Merchant, Nose Pickers	Reserves
Fifth Column	Enemy Spies and Saboteurs
52-20 Club	20 Weeks of 52 dollars for unemployed vets
File 13	Waste basket
Flack Happy	Saw too much battle action
Flack Shack	Rest Home
Flyin' the Hump	Himalayas
Frat Bait	Non-fraternization policy for G.I's. stationed in Germany. Didn't work, especially with the frauleins.
Flub the Dub	Foul up
FUBAR	Fucked Up Beyond All Repair
Fuck-off	A malingerer, one who hides from work
Fuck off	A term used to imply impatience, "Just get the hell out of here."
Fuck-up	One who screws up all tasks
Fuckin' A Right	Emphatic affirmative approval
Gibson Girl	Hand-cranked radio transmitter
Gizmo	Anything that could be labeled equally well as a watchamacallit or thingamagig, nonsense
Golden Gate in '48	Hoping for end of hostilities
Got A Dose	Venereal Disease
Gremlin	Any malfunction
Good Show	British for "Job well done" or good news

Hash Marks	Service stripes, Rank
Herman Nelson	Ventilator over galley
Heave Out and Lash Up	Get out of hammock and tie it up
Hit the Sack	Time for bed
Hollywood Delight	Grass Salad
Hubba Hubba	Get moving, or wow, look at that babe!
Jerry Can	German gas container
Jimmy Legs	Master at arms (policeman)
Jungle Juice	Liquor in the Pacific
Kaiser Coffin	Small "baby" aircraft carrier
Kamikaze	Japanese suicide pilot
Keep 'em Flying	Keep up the good work
KP	Kitchen Police - kitchen duty
K Rations	Nutritious (ugh) G.I. packaged food
Khaki Wacky	A girl who is crazy about military guys from any branch of service.
Kilroy Was Here	Mythical character appearing anywhere
Kraut	German soldier
Liberty Ships	Hastily built boats for war transport
Liberty, but no boats	No shore leave
Lili Marlene	German song adopted by the Allies
Loose Lips Sink Ships	Avoid voicing military information
Lord Haw Haw	Propaganda broadcaster from Germany
Luftwaffe	German Air Force
Maggies Drawers	On firing range, red flag indicates you missed
Manhattan Project	Atomic bomb research
Mail Call	Arrival of mail
Maytag Charlie	Nickname for Japanese aerial scout plane
Mail Buoy	No such thing; used to confuse rookie sailors
Merrill's Marauders	Volunteer missions under Gen. Frank Merrill
Messerschmitt	German aircraft manufacturer
Milk Run	Easy target
Moaning Minnie	Air raid sirens in London, also German shell, sometimes called Screaming Meemies
Mobilization	Call to arms
Molotov Cocktail	Hand made explosive device
Mudslinger	Infantryman
Mulberry	Artificial harbors, for D-Day Invasion
Nervous in the Service (for Brooklynites...Noivus in da Soivus)	
Ninety Day Wonder	Accelerated training for new officers
Nissen Huts	Also known as Quonset Huts

"No atheist in a fox hole"	Battle fear requires prayer
Nose Art	Paintings on nose of planes
OCS	Officer Candidate School
Oh My Achin' Back	Exclamation of dismay
Over the Hump	Flying over the Himalayas to India or China
Overlord	D-Day code name
Pass the Red Load	Catsup
Pencil Pusher	Navigator on plane or guy with desk job
Penis Machinist, Chancre Mechanic	Pharmacist Mate
Petty	Pin-up artist
PFC	Poor Fuckin' Civilian
Piccadilly Cowboy	Hangout for G.I.'s in London
Piccadilly Commando	Prostitute
Piss Call	Time to urinate
Piss Call Charlie	Awakened by enemy planes or gun fire
Piss off	Scram - get lost
Pissed off	Angry, annoyed
Piss poor	Expression of poor performance
Piss and Punk	Bread and water punishment
Pogey Bait	Candy
Police the Area	Clean up the crap
Points	Numerical quantity for rotation to states
Poop From The Group	Rumors from Group Headquarters
Prang	RAF slang, to bomb or to crash
Purple Heart Corner	Lowest flying element in bomber formation
Red Ball Express	Supply route from Normandy beaches
Repple Depple	Replacement Depot
Revetment	Hard embankment to protect planes
Rotation	Going back to the States
Ruptured Duck	Discharge button
Sack Time	Bed time
Sad Sack	Creation of Yank cartoonist George Baker
Scrambled Eggs	High naval officers' braid on caps
Screwed, Blewed and Tattoed	Getting a raw deal
Scuttlebutt	Latest rumors
Shape up or ship out	Perform better or get replaced
Shavetail	Army Second Lt.
SHAEF	Supreme Hdqs. Allied Expeditionary Forces
Shit Detail	Work detail, interference with leisure
Short Arm Inspection	Check-up for VD
Short Snorter	Exclusive club for flyers

"Sighted Sub - Sank Same"	Laconic message by Naval Commander
Slop Jockey	Mess cook, food server
Slop Chute	Mess Hall, Galley
Slop Slinger or Belly Robber	Cook
SNAFU	Situation Normal, All Fucked Up
SOS	Shit on a shingle, Chipped beef on toast
Sortie	Mission of single aircraft
Spread Your Cheeks	Position for inoculation shots
Stew Burner	Ship's cook
Spam	Most popular G.I. food
Squawk Sheet	Pilot's report of aircraft defects
Stateside	In the U.S.A.
Stillwell Rd.	Ledo-Burma road, named by Chiang Kai-Shek
Stupor Juice	A type of high powered booze devised by GI's in Normandy
Strafe	Fire at close range or from low flying aircraft
Tally-Ho	Enemy sighted and recognized
The Eagle Shits Today	Pay day
The G.I.'s	A case of diarrhea
Tokyo Rose	Propaganda broadcaster
Torch	Code name for invasion of North Africa
Torpedo Juice	Pure alcohol mixed with pineapple juice
T. S. Card	Tough shit, take your problem to the chaplain
U.S.O.	United Service Organization
Vargas	Pin-up artist
V-1, V-2	Jet propelled rocket bomb
V For Victory	Fingers forming letter "V"
Vinegar Joe	Nickname for General Stilwell
V Mail	"Victory Mail"...letters reduced in size
Werhrmacht	German Armed Forces
Willie and Joe	Infantrymen in Bill Mauldin's cartoons
Wolfpack	Groups of German submarines
Yank	American soldier
Yeoman	Company clerk
"You'll be sorry"	Sing-song expression denoting displeasure
Zippo	Most famous cigarette lighter

This is all I could come up with. Any more that your aging memories can revive will be added if we decide to have a second edition.

Songs, Poems & Jokes

Songs of the War Years...
When music was music

I've Heard That Song Before . . . . Harry James/Helen Forrest

Chattanooga Choo Choo . . . . Glenn Miller/Tex Beneke

Star Dust . . . . Artie Shaw/Billie Butterfield

You Made Me Love You . . . . Harry James

On The Sunny Side of the Street. . . . . Tommy Dorsey

Begin the Beguine . . . . Artie Shaw

I Can't Get Started With You . . . . Bunny Berrigan

There, I've Said It Again. . . . . Vaughn Monroe

Don't Be That Way . . . . Benny Goodman

Blues In The Night . . . . Woody Herman

Sunrise Serenade . . . . Glen Gray/Frankie Carle

Tangerine; Green Eyes . . . . Jimmy Dorsey/Bob Eberly/
                                                              Helen O'Connell

Daddy . . . . Sammy Kaye

In The Mood . . . . Glenn Miller

I'll Never Smile Again . . . . Tommy Dorsey/Frank Sinatra/
                                                              Pied Pipers

Deep Purple . . . . Larry Clinton/Bea Wain

Mood Indigo; Take the "A" Train . . . . Duke Ellington

Heartaches. . . . . Ted Weems/Elmo Tanner

Frenesi; Dancing In The Dark . . . . Artie Shaw

One O'Clock Jump . . . . Count Basie

Tuxedo Junction; Moonlight Serenade. . . . . Glenn Miller

Sing, Sing, Sing . . . . Benny Goodman/Harry James/
                                                              Gene Krupa

Skyliner; Cherokee. . . . . Charlie Barnett

Piano Concerto . . . . Freddy Martin/Jack Fina

Stompin' at the Savoy . . . . Benny Goodman

Night Train. . . . . Buddy Morrow

Three Little Fishes. . . . . Kay Kyser

Marie; Opus 1 . . . . Tommy Dorsey

Beat Me Daddy, Eight To The Bar . . . . Will Bradley/Ray McKinley

T'Ain't What You Do, It's The Way That You Do It. . . . Jimmie Lundsford

Got a Date With an Angel. Hal Kemp/Skinny Ennis

THE DOGFACE SOLDIER

Moderato

I WOULD-N'T GIVE A BEAN TO BE A FAN-CY PANTS MAR-INE

——I'D RA-THER BE A DOG-FACE SOL-DIER LIKE I

AM——; I WOULD-N'T TRADE MY OLD—O D's FOR

ALL THE NA-VY'S DUN-GA-REES FOR I'M THE WALK-ING

PRIDE OF UN-CLE SAM——; ON ALL THE POST-ERS THAT I

READ IT SAYS THE AR-MY BUILDS MEN——SO THEY'RE

TEAR-ING ME DOWN TO BUILD ME O-VER A-GAIN——I'M

JUST A DOG-FACE SOL-DIER WITH A RI-FLE ON MY

SHOUL-DER AND I EAT A KRAUT FOR BREAK-FAST E'V'RY DAY

——, SO FEED ME AM—MUN-I-TION, KEEP ME

IN THE THIRD DIV-I-SION , YOUR DOG-FACE SOL-DIER

BOY'S O———KAY.

At The Woodchopper's Ball . . . . Woody Herman

I've Got My Love To Keep Me Warm . . . . Les Brown

And The Angels Sing . . . . Benny Goodman/Martha Tilton

A String of Pearls . . . . Glenn Miller/Bobby Hackett

You'll Never Know . . . . Dick Haymes

I'll Be Seeing You . . . . Vera Lynn

Mairzy Doats . . . . Merry Macs

Rum and Coca Cola . . . . Andrews Sisters

Dance With A Dolly (With a Hole in Her Stocking) . . . . . Russ Morgan

Don't Fence Me In . . . . Bing Crosby/Andrew Sisters

Don't Get Around Much Anymore . . . . Ink Spots

You Always Hurt The One You Love . . . . Mills Brothers

Boogie Woogie Bugle Boy . . . . Andrew Sisters

To Each His Own . . . . Ink Spots

Swinging On A Star . . . . Bing Crosby

Coming In On A Wing And A Prayer . . . . Song Spinners

Shoo Shoo Baby . . . . Andrews Sisters

Ac-cent-chu-ate The Positive . . . . Bing Crosby/Andrew Sisters

Deep In The Heart Of Texas . . . . Bing Crosby

There Are Such Things . . . . T. Dorsey/F. Sinatra/Andrew Sisters

Don't Sit Under The Apple Tree . . . . Glenn Miller/Marion Hutton

As Time Goes By . . . . Rudy Vallee

Green Eyes . . . . Jimmy Dorsey/Bob Eberly/
                                                              Helen O'Connell

Till The End Of Time . . . . Perry Como

When The Lights Go On Again . . . . Vaughn Monroe

In The Mood . . . . Glenn Miller

I Left My Heart At The Stage Door Canteen . . . . Sammy Kaye

Chickery Chick . . . . Sammy Kaye

My Dreams Are Getting Better All The Time . . . . Les Brown/Doris Day

Saturday Night Is The Loneliest Night Of The Week . . . Frank Sinatra

Somebody Else Is Taking My Place . . . . Benny Goodman/Peggy Lee

I Don't Want To Set The World On Fire . . . . Horace Heidt

Praise The Lord And Pass The Ammunition . . . . Kay Kyser

I'll Get By . . . . Harry James

Oh, What It Seems To Be . . . . Frankie Carle/Marjorie Hughes

Pistol Packin' Mama . . . . Al Dexter

Jingle, Jangle, Jingle . . . . Kay Kyser/Harry Babbitt/Julie Conway

Sentimental Journey . . . . Les Brown/Doris Day

A
Christmas Prayer

Let us pray that strength and courage abundant be given to all who work for a world of reason and understanding ★ that the good that lies in every man's heart may day by day be magnified ★ that men will come to see more clearly not that which divides them, but that which unites them ★ that each hour may bring us closer to a final victory, not of nation over nation, but of man over his own evils and weaknesses ★ that the true spirit of this Christmas Season — its joy, its beauty, its hope, and above all its abiding faith — may live among us ★ that the blessings of peace be ours — the peace to build and grow, to live in harmony and sympathy with others, and to plan for the future with confidence.

Anon

It's Been A Long Long Time . . . . Harry James/Kitty Kalen

Always . . . . Deanna Durbin

Seems Like Old Times . . . . Guy Lombardo

Moonlight Becomes You . . . . Bing Crosby

My Devotion . . . . Vaughn Monroe

Lilli Marlene . . . . Perry Como

My Prayer . . . . Ink Spots

I Think Of You . . . . Tommy Dorsey

Sleepy Time Gal . . . . Harry James

Harbor Lights . . . . Francis Langford

My Buddy . . . . Sammy Kaye

Linda . . . . Buddy Clark

The Gypsy . . . . The Ink Spots

Embraceable You . . . . Jimmy Dorsey

Love Letters . . . . Dick Haymes

I Can't Begin To Tell You . . . . Harry James/Betty Grable

As Time Goes By . . . . Dooley Wilson

To Each His Own . . . . Eddy Howard

Miss You . . . . Dinah Shore

Five Minutes More . . . . Tex Beneke

Now Is The Hour . . . . Bing Crosby

Something to Remember You By . . . . Dinah Shore

You Are My Sunshine; Sioux City Sue . . . . Bing Crosby

Stardust . . . . Artie Shaw

Moonlight Cocktail . . . . Glenn Miller/Ray Eberle/
                                                                    The Modernaires

Paper Doll . . . . Mills Brothers

I Don't Want To Walk Without You . . . . Harry James/Helen Forrest

On The Sunny Side Of The Street . . . . Tommy Dorsey

I'll Be With You In Apple Blossom Time . . . . Andrew Sisters

Together . . . . Helen Forrest/Dick Haymes

All Or Nothing At All . . . . Frank Sinatra/Harry James

Rumors Are Flying . . . . Frankie Carle

Is You Is Or Is You Ain't Ma' Baby . . . . Bing Crosby

Shoo Fly Pie, Apple Pan Dowdy . . . . Dinah Shore

There Goes That Song Again . . . . Russ Morgan

Who Wouldn't Love You . . . . Kay Kyser

Jersey Bounce . . . . Benny Goodman

Candy . . . . Johnny Mercer/Jo Stafford/Pied Pipers

KEEP ON MARCHING

Keep on marching, always marching,
Though your footsteps start to slow
And your mouth is dry and parching
And your spirit's mighty low.

Keep on singing, always singing,
Though you want to cry "Enough!"
And you hear a hazy ringing
In your ears when things get tough.

Keeping on praying, always praying,
That your spirit won't unbend
And your heart and soul are saying,
"I'll keep on marching 'till the end. "

Straighten Up And Fly Right . . . . Nat King Cole

Amour . . . . Andy Russell

Till Then. . . . . Mills Brothers

We Three . . . . Ink Spots

My Heart Tells Me . . . . Glen Gray

Dream. . . . . The Pied Pipers

Long Ago And Far Away . . . . Helen Forrest/Dick Haymes

Amapola. . . . . Jimmy Dorsey/Bob Eberly/

Helen Forrest

Dolores . . . . Jimmy Dorsey/Frank Sinatra/

Pied Pipers

Twilight Time. . . . . Three Sons

I Hear A Rhapsody . . . . Charlie Barnett

God Bless America . . . . Kate Smith

If I Loved You. . . . . Perry Como

Symphony . . . . Freddie Martin

Sunday, Monday Or Always . . . . Bing Crosby

Blues In The Night . . . . Woody Herman

I'll Be Home For Christmas . . . . Bing Crosby

White Christmas . . . . Bing Crosby

Racing With The Moon. . . . . Vaughn Monroe

I Dream Of You . . . . Tommy Dorsey

I Had The Craziest Dream . . . . Harry James

One Dozen Roses . . . . Dick Jergens

Bell Bottom Trousers . . . . Tony Pastor

I've Got A Gal In Kalamazoo . . . . Glenn Miller/Marion Hutton/

Modernaires

Twilight Time. . . . . Three Sons

Pistol Packin' Mama . . . . Bing Crosby

Doctor, Lawyer, Indian Chief. . . . . Betty Hutton

The Christian Soldier's Hymn
(Tune : Rock of Ages)

Jesus captain of my soul, let me take a soldier's role;
I would join thy host for life,in thy ranks I'll ever fight,
Till life's battle all is done, and the field for thee is won.

Supply thou my every need, thy command I'll always heed;
While thy orders I obey, hear me as I fight and pray,
When into the fight I go, give me grace to meet the foe.

Dress me with thy armor Lord, it shall be my rich reward;
Arm me with thy mighty sword, conquer with thy Holy Word,
Give me faith for a shield, lest to satan's darts I yield.

Thy helmet of salvation done, will assure the victory won;
Righteousness to clothe my breast, girded with truthfulness,
Swift I'll bring thy news of peace, with thy sandals on my feet.

Jesus captain of my soul, when the battle all is done;
And the glorious victory's won, may I hear thee say " Well Done",
Thou hast fought the goodly fight, enter in to Eternal Life.
Amen.

Rev. Luke H. Turner
WW-2 D.A.V. Purple Heart

DICK HAYMES FAVORITES

You'll Never Know; Little White Lies; The More I See You; Where Or When; It Might As Well Be Spring; It Had To Be You; Together; How Deep Is The Ocean; Till The End Of Time; Laura; It's Magic; Mam'selle; The Nearness Of You; Moonlight Becomes You; The Very Thought Of You; I'll Buy That Dream; They Didn't Believe Me; I Only Have Eyes For You; Oh! What It Seemed To Be; The Girl ThatI Marry; I'll Get By.

SPIKE JONES...THE MAN WHO MURDERED MUSIC

Cocktails For Two; The William Tell Oveture; Der Fuhrer's Face; I Waz a Wabbit; Hawaiian War Chant; Carmen; The Man On The Flying Trapeze; Tennessee Walk; Chloe; Gesundheit Polka; Riders In The Sky; Liebestraum; Yes, We Have No Bananas; You Always Hurt The One You Love; The Sheik Of Araby; The Glow Worm; My Old Flame; Holiday For Strings; Laura; Love In Bloom; That Old Black Magic; All I Want For Christmas Is My Two Front Teeth

SONGS OF VERA LYNN

The Bells Of St. Mary's; The Anniversary Waltz; I'll Be With You In Apple Blossom Time; The White Cliffs Of Dover; Yours; Something To Remember You By; Maybe; When The Lights Go On Again; Wishing; Be Careful; It's My Heart; Mexicali Rose; I Don't Want To Set The World On Fire; We'll Meet Again.; I'll Be Seeing You

DINAH SHORE FAVORITES

I'll Walk Alone; Buttons and Bows; Dear Hearts And Gentle People; You'd Be So Nice To Come Home To; The Anniversary Song; I Wish I Didn't Love You So Much; For Sentimental Reasons; My Heart Cries For You; Laughing On The Outside; Baby, It's Cold Outside; It's So Nice To Have A Man Around The House; Doin' What Comes Naturally; I Don't Want To Walk Without You; Blues In The Night; A Penny A Kiss; Miss You; Sweet Violets; Something to Remember You By; I'll Be Seeing You.

THE FOURTH OF JULY

John Pierpont

Day of glory! Welcome day!
Freedom's banners greet thy ray;
See! how cheerfully they play
  With thy morning breeze,
On the rocks where pilgrims kneeled,
On the heights where squadrons wheeled,
When a tyrant's thunder pealed
  O'er the trembling seas.

God of armies! did thy stars
On their courses smite his cars;
Blast his arm, and wrest his bars
  From the heaving tide?
On our standards! lo! they burn.
And, when days like this return,
Sparkle o'er the soldier's urn
  Who for freedom died.

God of peace! whose spirit fills
All the echoes of our hills,
All the murmur of our rills,
  Now the storm is o'er,
O let freemen be our sons,
And let future Washingtons
Rise, to lead their valiant ones
  Till there's war no more!

THE BRITISH GIRL'S LAMENT

Dear old England, not the same,
   The dreaded invasion, well it came,
But no, its not the beastly hun,
   The Dam Ol' Yankee army's come.

You'll see them in the trams and bus,
   There isn't room for both of us,
We walk to let them have our seats,
   Then get run over by their Jeeps.

They moan about our lukewarm beer,
   Think beer's like water over here,
But after drinking two or more,
   You'll find them lying on the floor.

And you should see them try to dance,
   They find a partner, try to prance,
When you're half dead they stop and smile,
   "How'm I doing, Honey Chile".

With admiration we would stare,
   At all the ribbons that they wear,
And think of deeds both bold and daring,
   That earned the medals they are wearing.

Alas, they haven't fought the hun,
   No glorious battles have they won,
That pretty ribbon just denotes,
   They've crossed the sea - brave men in boats.

They say that they can shoot and fight,
   It's true they fight - yes - when they're tight,
I must admit their shootings fine,
   They shoot a dam good Yankee line.

They tell you you've got teeth like pearls,
   They love your hair, the way it curls,
Your eyes would dim the brightest star,
   You're competition for Hedy Lamarr.

You are their love, their life, their all,
   And for no other girl could they ever fall,
They'll love you dear 'til death do part,
   And if you leave it'll break their heart.

And then they'll leave you broken hearted,
   The camp has moved - your love departed,
You'll wait for mail that doesn't come,
   Then you'll realize, you're awful dumb.

In a different town - a different place,
   To a different girl - a different face,
"I love you darling, please be mine",
   It's the same old Yank, the same old line.
American War Office - 1944

Lili Marlen

Outside the barracks, by the corner light,
I'll always stand and wait for you at night.
We will create a world for two,
I'd wait for you, the whole night through
For you, Lili Marlen, for you Lili Marlen.

Bugler, tonight don't play the call to arms,
I want another evening with her charms.
Then we must say goodbye and part.
I'll always keep you in my heart
With me, Lili Marlen, with me Lili Marlen.

Give me a rose to show how much you care,
Tie to the stem a lock of golden hair.
Surely tomorrow you'll feel blue,
But then will come a love that's new
For you, Lili Marlen, for you, Lili Marlen.

When we are marching in the mud and cold,
And when my pack seems more than I can hold,
My love for you renews my might,
I'm warm again, my pack is light.
It's you, Lili Marlen, it's you, Lili Marlen.

Was there a real Lilli Marlene, the darling of that song that swept the ETO during World War II and was adopted by millions of combat troops on both sides?

Lilli was the sex symbol of the American GI, the British Tommy, the goosestepping Wehrmacht and other soldiers in the theater—a personification of that wife, or sweetheart who waited back home.

She was the gal whose plaintive song topped the Hit Parade and the record charts all over the European theater. She was the lass who waited "Underneath the lantern, by the barrack gate" for her man's return.

Lilli— They All Loved Her

By Charles R. Byrnes

As the story goes, the song originally was property of the Germans. It was captured by the British in North Africa and the Americans were quick to take it over as did other armies engaged in the conflict. It was adapted in 19 languages and went the rounds.

It was strange that American GIs—reared on a diet of swing dished out by Benny Goodman, Glenn Miller and the Dorseys, to name only the most notable—liked the almost dirgelike tune. But that they did and the slow-moving sing mirrored their feelings at being thousands of miles from home and engaged in deadly combat.

It was a huge favorite on American and British radio stations that aired news and music to the embattled troops. And the tune was a regular on powerful Nazi networks.

It has taken almost 40 years to reveal the facts behind the song that far surpassed in popularity the risque "Mademoiselle from Armentieres" of World War I.

Actually, there wasn't a Lilli Marlene. The melody came from the Serbian infantry march by Yugoslav composer Mirko Silic. The words were from a poem written by a World War I German soldier.

The two were merged in April 1941, according to Silic, who then worked for the recording studios of the Yugoslav Broadcasting Service. Fearing an imminent Nazi invasion, the Yugoslav government commissioned hi to compose a martial them for propaganda purposes.

Silic changed the original tun a bit and admittedly took elements from another written by a German composer.

As tension mounted between the Yugoslavs and Germans, the song was aired Sunday afternoon, April 6, the day the anticipated onslaught began. In the morning the Luftwaffe subjected Belgrade to an all out bombing. Shortly afterward, Nazi tanks and infantry blitzed across the border, captured the city and Radio Belgrade.

The Nazis immediately put the powerful transmitter back on the air, but discovered all the station's phonograph records had been shattered., with the exception of Silic's new march. As a result, it was played continuously as background for German propaganda.

On the heels of the invasion, the Nazis flew in a blond cabaret singer, Lale Andersen, to entertain their troops. She immediately liked the music, but decided it needed words. Lale was aware that a German poem, Hans Leip's "Lilli Marlene" was one of Hitler's favorites. So with the help of Silic and others, she slowed down the tempo and added Leip's words.

Fraulein Andersen introduced the song on the station April 21. It was an instant hit with German troops.

The song was recorded and became the theme song of the Nazi controlled radio station. And singer Andersen made a lifelong career off Lilli Marlene that continued until her death in 1972.

Poet Hans Leip has since revealed that his words dated back to World War I when he was a soldier in Berlin. Doing sentry duty near a military hospital, he became enamored of two German girls who daily passed his post. One was name Marlene, the other Lilli.

The talented Leip wrote three verses about the girls, but merged them into one—Lilli Marlene. His poem was published in 1917 in a Berlin newspaper and was reprinted in an anthology in the late 1930s.

There were several English versions. Typically, the Yanks shortened the name to "Lilli" and their adaption differed from others, although the melody was uniform. The British warriors had their own.

Thus a song that spanned two world wars became the adopted ballad of the second.

Few of the millions of combat soldiers engaged in World War II ever knew or probably cared where it originated. It provided them with entertainment and took their thoughts back home where loved ones waited.

Still More Songs...

Love Walked In

Jim

The Anniversary Waltz

Let There Be Love

Alice Blue Gown

When The Swallows Come Back To Capistrano

Dinah

Is It True What They Say About Dixie?

Miss You

Tattletale

The Woodpecker Song

I Don't Want To Set The World On Fire

These Foolish Things Remind Me Of You

Do I Worry?

Music Makers

Sam, You Made The Pants Too Long

The Things I Love

I Guess I'll Have To Dream The Rest

Yes Indeed

Kiss The Boys Goodbye

My Sister And I

It's So Peaceful In The Country

Tuxedo Junction

The Breeze And I

You Walk By

B'ye Now

It's A Sin To Tell A Lie

Five O'Clock Whistle

Two Dreams Met

Flamingo

Perfidia

The Nearness Of You

The Band Played On

I Married An Angel

Six Lessons From Madam LaZonga

Playmates

Without A Song

Yours

I Came, I Saw, I Conquered

Who

You Are My Sunshine

A Sinner Kissed An Angel

Just A Little Bit South Of North Carolina

God Bless America

The Bad Humor Man

The Same Old Story

I'm Nobody's Baby

Arthur Miller Taught Me Dancing

Dear Mom

We Did It Before

On The Street Of Regret

Make Love To Me

I Didn't Know What Time It Was

Imagination

Ferryboat Serenade

I Said No

Mandy Is Two

Wait Till The Sun Shines, Nellie

Sleepy Lagoon

Winter Weather

Sometimes

She'll Always Remember

I've Got A Date With A Dream

Walkin' By The River

You Got Me This Way

This Love Of Mine

Why Don't We Do This More Often?

The Lamplighter's Serenade

Someone Else Is Taking My Place

Breathless

Someone's Rockin' My Dreamboat

Goody-Goody

Let's Face The Music

You Are My Lucky Star

Alone

I'm Putting All My Eggs In One Basket

Blues In The Night

Everything Happens To Me

Do You Care?

I'm Stepping Out With A Memory Tonight

May I Never Love Again

I Understand

Our Love Affair

The Last Time I Saw Paris

If It's True

The Hut-Sut Song

We Three

The Way You Look Tonight

You'll Never Know

Blueberry Hill

Says My Heart

A Rose And A Prayer

When Did You Leave Heaven?

Jealous

Buckle Down Winsocki

Intermezzo

Yes, My Darling Daughter

The Shrine Of St. Cecilia

I Remember You

Oh, Lady Be Good

I Got It Bad And That Ain't Good

Till Reveille

You And I

Five O'Clock Whistle

Time Was

Twenty One Dollars A Day, Once A Month

Only Forever

I Know Why

I'm Gonna Sit Right Down And Write Myself
    A Letter

Let's Get Away From It All

A Nightingale Sang In Barkeley Square

Two In Love

Moonlight Masquerade

You Stepped Out Of A Dream

I'm An Old Cowhand

Aurora

Blues In The Night

Everything Happens To Me

I Don't Want To Walk Without You

Do I Care?

I'm Always Chasing Rainbows

South Of The Border

Hold Tight

Lilacs In The Rain

Blue Orchids

Thanks For The Memory

Scatterbrain

Penny Serenade

Rose O'Day

Not Mine

In The Mood

Somebody Loves Me

This Is No Laughing Matter

Sentimental Journey

I'll Be Around

He Wears A Pair Of Silver Wings

Pennsylvania Polka

On The Street Of Regret

I'm Glad There Is You

Wonder When My Baby's Coming Home

Just As Though You Were Here

If You Are But A Dream

At Last

We'll Meet Again

Somebody Else Is Taking My Place

I Left My Heart At The Stagedoor Canteen

Not Mine

Remember Pearl Harbor

Johnny Doughboy

Paper Doll

Sweet Eloise

Do You Miss Your Sweetheart?

Dearly Beloved

I Came Here To Talk For Joe

Yankee Doodle Dandy

What Does A Soldier Dream Of?

Three Little Sisters

Always In My Heart

White Christmas

My Devotion

Strip Polka

Pretty Little Busybody

I'll Be Around

Every Night About This Time

Be Careful, It's My Heart

I Got A Gal In Kalamazoo

Serenade In Blue

At Last

Jingle Jangle

My Devotion

He's My Guy

This Is Worth Fighting For

One Dozen Roses

Poor You

My Little Cousin

The Very Thought of You

This is the Army

So how many of these oldies can you old fogies hum or sing the words to? Care to contribute for future updated versions of our musical journey through memory lane?
Just drop me a line.

Service Songs

ARMY AIR CORPS

WILD BLUE YONDER

1.

Off we go, into the wild blue yonder,

Flying high, into the sun;

Here they come, zooming to meet our thunder,

At 'em boys, give 'em the gun!

Down we dive, spouting our flames from under,

Off with one hell of a roar!

We live in fame or go down in flames;

Hey, nothing can stop the Army Air Corps!

Here's a toast to the host of those men who love
   the vastness of the sky;

To a friend we send a message of his brother
   men who fly.

We drink to those who gave their all of old,

Then down we roar to score the rainbow's pot
   of gold.

A toast to the host of men we boast, the Army
   Air Corps.

2.

Minds of men fashioned a crate of thunder,

Sent it high into the blue;

Hands of men blasted the world asunder;

How they lived God only knew!

Souls of men dreaming of skies to conquer

Gave us wings ever to soar.

With scouts before and bombers galore,

Nothing'll stop the Army Air Corps!

3.

Off we go into the wild blue younder,

Keep the wings level and true.

If you'd live to be a grey haired wonder,

Keep the nose out of the blue!

Flying men guarding the Nation's border,

We'll be there followed by more.

In echelon we carry on,

Nothing will stop the Army Air Corps

ARMY

THE CAISSONS GO ROLLING ALONG

Over hill over dale,

We have hit the dusty trail,

And those Caissons go rollin' along.

"Counter March! Right about!"

Hear those wagon soldiers shout,

While those Caissons go rolling along.

For it's Hi! Hi! Hee! In the field artillery,

Call off your numbers loud and strong! (Call
   off!)

And where e'er we go, you will always know

That those caissons are rolling along; (Keep
   'em rolling!)

That those caissons are rolling along. For it's

Hi! Hi! hee! In the field artillery,

Call off your numbers loud and strong! (Call
   off!)

And where e'er we go, you will always know

That those caissons are rolling along; (Keep
   'em rolling!)

That those caissons are rolling along

2.

To the Front, day and night,

Where the doughboys dig and fight,

And those caissons go rolling along.

Our barrage will be there

Fired on the rocket's glare,
Where those caissons go rollin' along.

SONG OF THE ARMY ENGINEER

1.

The Engineer's "Embattled Banners,"
In spirit born at Bunker Hill,
A living flame at Cerro Gordo,
Has carried on through Saint Mihiel.

Refrain:

Guardian of the Nation's birthright,
"Freedom's foreward fighting line,
"On the fighting line,
The spirit of "Embattled Banners,"
Forever more shall brightly shine.
2.
The Captain says my rifle's rusty,
And I don't know but what he's right,
 (Sure he's right)
If he'd inspect my pick and shovel,
He'd always find them shining bright

Refrain:

Shining brightly in the moonlight,
Always find them shining bright,
Shining brightly and O, yes!
That handy pick and shovel,
He'd always find them shining bright.
3.
The sergeant says to K.P. Bunko,
And I don't know but what he's right,
 (Sure he's right)
You may be tops at engineering,
But son, you shine those dishes bright.

Refrain:

Shining brightly in the moonlight,
Always keep them shining bright,

Shining brightly and O, yes!
You're tops at engineering,
But son, you shine those dishpans bright.

NAVY

ANCHORS AWEIGH

1.

Anchors Aweigh, my boys, anchors Aweigh.
Farewell to college joys, we sail at break of day-
 day-day -day!
Through our last night on shore, drink to the
 foam,
Until we meet once more here's wishing you a
 happy voyage home.

Heave a-ho there, sailor, ev'rybody drink up
 while you may,
Heave a-ho there, sailor, for you're gonna sail at
 break of day,
Drink away, drink away, for you sail at break of
 day, hey!
2.
Stand, Navy, down the field, sail to the sky,
We'll never change our course; so Army, you
 steer shy-y-y-y,
Roll up the score, Navy, Anchors Aweigh,
Sail, Navy, down the field and sink the Army,
 sink the Army, sink the Army Grey.
3.
"Stand, Army, to the bar, raise your glasses
 high;
We'll never pay the bill so Navy you must buy-
 buy-buy-buy, down
Gordon Gin, Army; down Rock and Rye;
Stand, Army, to the bar and drink the Navy,
 drink the Navy dry."

MARINES

FROM THE HALLS OF MONTEZUMA

1.

From the halls of Montezuma
To the shores of Tripoli,
We fight our country's battles
On the land and on the sea.
First to fight for right and freedom
And to keep our honor clean,
We are proud to claim the title
Of United States Marine.

2.

Our flag's unfurled to every breeze
From dawn to setting sun.
We have fought in every clime and place
Where we could take a gun.
In the snow of far off Northern lands
And in sunny tropic scenes
Your will find us always on the job...
The United States Marines.

3.

Here's health to you and to our Corps
Which we are proud to serve.
In many a strife we've found for life
And never lost our nerve.
If the Army and the Navy
Ever look on heaven's scenes
They will find the streets are guarded
By the United States Marines.

ENGLISH (LIMEY) DITTIES

(Limeys got their name from the use of lime to prevent scurvy on long ocean voyages.)

FUCK (BLESS) THEM ALL.

If expletive words disturb your sensitive sensibilities, you may substitute the "blessed" sanitized version.

They say there's a troop ship just leaving
    Bombay,
Bound for old Blighty shore,
Heavily laden with tired men,
Bound for the land they adore.
There's many an airman just finishing his time,
Many a bloke signing on
But you get no promotions this side of the
    ocean
So cheer up me lads, fuck 'em all...

Fuck 'em all, fuck 'em all
The long, the short and the tall
Fuck all the sergeants and WO 1's (warrant
    offficer 1)
Fuck all the corporals and their bastard sons
So we're saying good-bye to them all, an' back
    to our barracks we crawl,
There'll be no promotions this side of the ocean
So cheer up me lads...Fuck 'em all.

ROLL ME OVER

Roll me over, in the clover, roll me over, lay me
    down and do it again,
For this is number one an' the fun has just
    begun
Roll me over, lay me down and do it again.
For this is number two and he's got me in a
    stew

Roll me over, lay me down and do it again.

And this in number three and his hand is on my knee,

Roll me over, lay me down and do it again.

For this is number four, and he's got me on the floor,

Roll me over, lay me down and do it again.

And this is number five, and his hand is on my thigh,

Roll me over, lay me down and do it again.

For this is number six, and he's got me in a fix,

Roll me over, lay me down and do it again.

This is number seven, and it's just like being in heaven,

Roll me over, lay me down and do it again.

Now this is number eight and the doctor's at the gate,

Roll me over, lay me down and do it again.

And this is number nine, and the twins are doing fine,

Roll me over, lay me down and do it again.

Now this number ten, and he wants to start again,

Roll me over...lay me down... and do it again.

Other versions:

1 And it was so much fun

2 It was the greatest screw

3 I couldn't even see

4 An' I kept begging for more

5 I'm glad I'm so alive

What the British used to say about us:

The Yanks are overpaid...over sexed...and over here!

BELL BOTTOM TROUSERS

Once I was service maid, down in Drewry Lane

My mother was so hard to me, my mistress was the same,

Then along came a sailor, home from the sea,

And he was the cause of all my misery.

He asked me for a candle, to light up the bed

Then asked me for a kerchief to tie around his head

And I like a silly girl, thinkin' it no harm

Slipped into the sailor's bed to keep the sailor warm,

Early in the mornin', before the break of day

He handed me a one pound note, and this to me did say,

Maybe you'll have a daughter, maybe you'll have a son

Take this my darling, for the damage I have done

If you have a daughter, bounce her on your knee,

But if you have a son, send the bastard out to sea,

Now the moral of this story is very plain to see

Never trust a sailor, an inch above your knee.

Version # Two

Oh, I was a bar maid, down in Drurys Lane

My master was so kind to me, my mistress was the same,

Along came a sailor, as happy as can be,

Now he is the cause, of all my misery...

Singing bell botton trousers, coats of navy blue,

He'll climb her riggings, like his daddy used to do,

Oh, he asked me for a kerchief, to tie around his head,

He asked me for a candle, to see his way to bed,

Singing Bell bottom....etc.

Now silly maid that I was, thinkin' it no harm,

Climbed into the sailor's bed, to keep the

sailor warm.

Singing Bell ....etc.

Oh, early in the mornin', he woke me from my bed,

He handed me a five pound note and this is what he said,

Take this me darlin', for the damage I have done,

Now if the baby is a girl, bounce her on you knee,

But if the baby is a boy, send the bastard out to sea

Singing ....etc

Now the moral of this story is plain as plain can be,

Never trust a sailor an inch above your knee.

I'VE GOT SIXPENCE

I've got sixpence, jolly jolly sixpence, I've got sixpence, to last me all me life,

I've got tuppence to spend, an' tuppence to lend an' tuppence to send home to my wife, poor wife,...

What joys have I to grieve me, and happy little girls to deceive me,

I'm happy as a king, believe me, As I go rolling, rolling home,

Rolling home, rolling home, by the light of the silveryyyy moooon

I'm as happy as a king, believe me, As I go rolling, rolling home.

WE JUST WANNA GO HOME

The coffee that they serve us, they say is mighty fine,

Good for cuts and bruises, tastes like (better than) iodine,

Oh, we don't want no more of Army life,

We just wanna go, we just wanna go, home.

The chicken that they feed us, they say is the very best,

We get the neck and assholes, the officers get the rest

Oh, we don't want....

The pancakes that they feed us, they say is mighty fine,

One fell off the table, and killed a friend of mine,

JOKES PLAYED ON RECRUITS...

"Bring in the firing line"

"Send the recruits to swim at the Motor Pool"

ODE TO CANNED COW

No tits to pull

No hay to pitch

Just punch a hole

In the son-of-a-bitch

THE PARATROOPERS SONG....

I'm sitting here and thinking
    Of the friends I left behind,
And it's hard to put on paper
    What's running through my mind.
We've packed a thousand parachutes
    And rode them to the ground.
We've drunk the beer and whiskey
    From every joint in town.
But there is a consolation
    Gather 'round me while I tell,
Cause when we die, we'll go to heaven
    For we've done our bitch in hell.

We've washed a million mess kits
    We've peeled a million spuds,
And we've marched a million miles
    In our heavy, muddy duds.

We've killed a million woodticks
    We've made a million camps,
We've pulled all the Georgia cactus
    From the seat of our god-damn pants.
But when the work is finished
    Then friends behind will tell,
"When they died, they went to heaven
    For they did their bitch in hell."

We've been awakened in the morning
    At an hour to try the soul,
And now and then a flashlight
    Was used to call the roll.

A corporal gripes a little bit
    The sergeant gripes some more
And by the time the captain starts
    We all are pretty sore.

But when the final tap has blown
    And we've laid aside our cares,
Then we'll stand our last inspection
On the shinning golden stairs.

Old St. Peter with his beard of white
    Will gaze upon us from his height,
"Have a rest you Jumpers," he will yell
    "You've done your bitch in hell."
        Contributed by Joseph Romas, Syracuse, N.Y.

INFANTRY SONG
What do you do in the infantry, you march, you
    march, you march,
What do you do in the infantry, when your back
    gets stiff as starch,
There's many a fall in the Cavalry, but never a
    fallen arch,
So what do you do in the infantry, you march,
    you march, you march.

There's many a fall in the Cavalry,
But never a fallen army
So what to you do in the infantry—you march
    you march, you march.

FROM A CAVALRY SOLDIER:
There'll be no piss call while in the saddle.
A good trooper can piss from horseback and
not get one drop on his breeches.

BARRACKS HUMOR:
    After lights out one night, the subject turned
to women. Talking about his escapades back in
West Virginia, this fellow said,
    "Man, back home I had me a little young gal,
and she was so tight.
    Every time I pulled out, her ass would suck
up the bedsheets."

SERVICE EXPERIENCE:
    I was a sniper in the 504th Parachute Infan-
try Regiment in the 82nd Airborne Division. I
parachuted during the Sicily invasion, Salerno
Italy invasion. I Jumped into Holland and made
water landings into Anzio, and by truck into the
Battle of the Bulge.
    But what happened up in the hills of Italy was
funny. I took out a patrol and visually picked out
a spot to get some good cover for us to get a
clean sight on a target for the next morning. I
brought my patrol back to our lines and went
back to the place I would set up for the early
morning. I spied a farm house building that was
shelled by the 504th and also by the kraut
artillery. The building had trees behind that I
could use for concealment, to back my tracks
after I got my shots off.
    About 4:00 a.m. I dozed off for about twenty
minutes to give my eyes a rest. Well, to my

surprise, (I didn't know it then) a cow decided to lay over my fox hole. I awoke, and couldn't move as the cow completely covered the hole. I punched and hit this thing and finally got my trench knife out and was sticking this thing. It started to bleed and it bled all over me, and wouldn't stop. I really got worried by this time as daybreak approached and I was in enemy territory. After an agonizing three hours, this big thing decided it had to be milked and finally got up.

I was in a bad spot as it was now daylight. I slowly took stock and crawled into the woods behind me and made my way back to our lines. Need I tell you, that cow saved me as 350 yards away was a Kraut officer open latrine and an easy target for a sniper. The medics looked at all the blood on me and thought I was bleeding to death.

ED MORAN, 504th Infantry Regiment

We had just driven the Krauts out of a small town in Luxembourg and taken occupancy of some houses where we captured some gritty looking enemy. After repelling a couple of counterattacks, we relaxed a bit and I was volunteered to guard four of them in this store-room.

There was a couple of barrels filled with apples. One of the Krauts motioned to me about "essen apfels...", and pointed to the barrels. I hesitated, but I nodded OK, my being the good samaritan.

They got to their feet and started to approach the barrels. My platoon Sgt. Sifkin, noticed this movement from the next room, and came storming in, screaming at the prisoners, threatening them with his carbine, and with a couple of swift kicks knocked the barrels over.

Not only did the "appfels" fall all over the room but some grenades and a machine pistol or two. How close to meeting the end of my days in my baptism of fire that day, I'll never know. I thank my lucky stars that I was with a bunch of veteran combat infantrymen who helped and guided me through my first weeks of combat.

Contributed by Abraham Lashin, Co. K 319 Inf. 80 Inf. Div.

WACs TALKING ABOUT THEIR XMAS PARTY:

First says while giggling, "I put a condom on our C.O.'s desk yesterday."

Second says, "I saw it and put a hole in it."

First one fainted.

LAY YOUR PISTOL DOWN

I went with a pistol packin' momma. All she wanted to do was get loaded!

THAT'S ENGLAND

When the heavenly dew whips thru the breeze
And you walk thru mud up to your knees,
Where the sun doesn't shine and the rain falls
    free,
And the fog is so thick you can hardly see.
That's England.

Where you live on brussel sprouts and Spam
And powdered eggs that ain't worth a damn
In town you only get Fish and Spuds
And down the taste with a mug of suds,
That's England

You hold your nose when you gulp it down
It hurts your stomach and then you frown,
For it burns your tongue, makes your throat
    feel queer

It's rightly named bitters, for it sure ain't beer.
That's England

Where the prices are high and ever so long
And those GI's are always, always wrong,
Your get watered scotch at four bits a snort
And those limey babes sure don't fall short.
That's England

And those pitch black nights when you stay out
    late
It's so bloody dark, you can't navigate.
There's no transportation, so you'll have to hike
And get your tail knocked off by a god-damn
    bike.
That's England

Where most of the girls are bland and bold
And think a Yank's pockets are lined with gold,
There's those Picadilly Commandos with
    painted allure
Steer clear of them, mate, or you're burned for
    sure.
That's England

This island ain't worth saving, I don't think
So cut loose the balloons and let the damn
    thing sink,
I ain't complaining, but I'll have you know
Life is rougher than hell in the ETO.
THAT'S ENGLAND

G.I. THIS AND G.I. THAT!
Sitting on my G.I. bed
My G.I. hat upon my head
My G.I. pants, my G.I. shoes
Everything free, nothing to lose.
They issue everything we need
Paper to write, books to read,

Your belt, your shoes, your G.I. tie.
Everything free, nothing to buy.
You eat your food from G.I. plates,
Fill your needs at G.I. rates,
It's G.I. this and G.I. that
G.I. haircut, G.I. hat
G.I. razor, G.I. comb
G.I. wish that I was home.

Greatest War Song Ever Written:
Here Comes The Bride

Shotgun marriage:
Outpost
A military wedding

British sentry - "Halt, who goes there?"
Soldier - "British soldiers."
British sentry - "Pass British soldiers."
British sentry - "Halt, who goes there?"
Soldier - "French soldiers."
British sentry - "Pass, French soldiers."
British sentry - "Halt, who goes there?"
Soldier - "Who the hell wants to know?"
British sentry - "Pass, Yanks."

Definition of a WAC
A double breasted soldier with a built-in fox-hole

G.I. Joe
Here lies my sergeant
Here let him lie
Now he's found rest
And so have I.

An Infantry idea of a kiss
First a reconnaissance, then a meeting
    engagement
Followed by a double envelopement and contact

Maintaining heavy pressure upon objective.
Then fire!

Short Arm:
Stand at attention and don't salute
Down with your pants and out with your root,
Milk it down, give it a squeeze,
Back in your pants, and stand at ease.

82nd Airborn
I am one jump ahead of the MP's, said the parachuter —As he pulled the rip chord.

Mudslinger
I know that I shall never see
A slit trench deep enough for me,
During every barrage while in my sleeper
I know tomorrow, I shall dig it deeper,
All through the night I hope and pray
That in the morning I can walk away.

G.I. Dittie
I am glad that I am an American
And I am glad that I am free
I wish that I was a great dane,
And Hitler was a tree.

Intellect
A dumb rookie...is one who thinks that a maneuver is something that you put on grass to make it grow.

Patriotism
Matilda the patriotic hen, lays bomb shaped eggs every other day.

Here's Mud in Your Eye
It was so muddy in France, you had to jack a cow up to milk it.

G.I. Wisdom
You can tell a private by his look of great alarm
You can always tell a sergeant by the chevrons on his arm,
You'll know a 1st. Lt. by his manner, dress and such
But with a new 2nd. Louie, you CAN'T tell HIM very much.

Theme song of the German Army:
Don't Get Around Much Anymore

Advice to G.Is who enter latrines:
1. G.I.'s with short rifles, stand within firing range.
2. Pilots with short engine mounts, taxi up close.

G.I. Gab
First G.I. - "Where did you get the German helmet?"
Second G.I. - "Had to kill twenty krauts to get it."
First G.I. - "How come?"
Second G.I. - "Wanted to get my exact size.

Famous words in the ETO
.Let's walk around the block a few times until the pub opens.

Wife - "If I die first, what will you put on my gravestone?"
Husband - "Here lies Sophie, cold as usual."
Husband - "And if I die first, what will you say?"
Wife - "Here lies Peter, stiff at last."

Lilly From Piccadilly

I took a trip to London, to look around the town

When I got to Piccadilly, the sun was going
down,

I never saw such darkness, the night was black
as pitch

When suddenly in front of me, I thought I saw a
witch.

Chorus:

Oh, it was Lilly From Piccadilly

You know the one I mean

I'll spend each pay day

That's my hey-hey day

With Lilly, my blackout-out queen.

I could not see her figure, I could not see her
face,

But if I ever meet her, I'll know her any place,

I could not tell if she was blonde or dark
Brunette

But gosh, oh gee, did she give me,

A thrill I won't forget.

Chorus:

They talk of Dirty Gerty, and say mademoiselle
in French,

But give me a Commando, in a foxhole or a
trench,

And in the thick of battle, you'll find me happy
there

But say chum be sure she comes

From Piccadilly square.

And when my children ask me, "Please tell
me daddy dear,

What did you do to win the war?" I'll answer
with a sneer,

"Your daddy was a hero, his best he always
fought

With bravery he gave his all, to the Commando his support."

Draft Notice

During the days of the draft McCormick
received his notice and was told to bring a urine
sample to the Selective Service Headquarters.

Figuring on outfoxing the draft board, the
Irishman filled a bottle with urine from his
father, girlfriend, and dog, and then added some
of his own. After turning in the sample,
McCormick waited for about a half hour.

Finally, the lab technician came out. "According to our lab tests," he reported, "your father
has diabetes, your girlfriend is pregnant, your
dog is in heat, and you're in the army."

Adolf Hitler said to Mae West:

"If a nickel is a nickel

And a dime is a dime,

Can I come up and see you some time?"

May West to Adolph Hitler:

"If a nickel is a nickel,

And a dime is a dime,

There are more after your ass

Than there are after mine."

**Last three pages contributed by George
Homiak, self-proclaimed mayor of Mt.
Carmel, PA.**

THE MARAUDER SONG

Sung to the tune of Ivan Stravinsky Skivar
(Beau Geste)

Oh, why did I join the Air Corps?
Mother, dear mother knew best;
Now here I lie 'neath the wreckage,
Maurauder all over my chest.

Chorus:

The Marauder's a very fine airplane,
Constructed of rivets and tin,
With a top speed of over three hundred
The ship with the headwind built in.

Chorus:

Oh, if you should go on a mission
With plenty of money to burn,
Any old crew chief will bet you
Two to one that you'll never return.

Chorus:

Oh, if you should run into trouble
And don't know which way to turn,
Just reach right up on the dashboard—
Push the button marked "Spin, Crash, and
Burn."

Chorus:

Oh, if you should run into ack-ack
Or a Messerschmidt makes a good pass,
Just shove back your seat and start walkin'—
To hell with the crew, save your ass.

Chorus:

Oh, if you've got in sixty missions
And have your orders for home,
Don't hang around for promotion—
They'll fly your ass back over Rome.

Chorus:

Oh, if you've got in sixty missions
And haven't developed a twitch,
Next time you hit Orvieto
You can skip-bomb the son of a bitch

Gerald Rasilke
Irving, Texas

An American sergeant, who probably was penning a poem titled "When Duty Calls" just about the time that John L. Lewis was preparing a strike call, was killed at his post as a waist gunner with a Flying Fortress crew in a bombing raid of the Northwest Africa Air Force. The following poem was found in his personal effects, and was forwarded to the Africa **Stars and Stripes** by his commanding officer:

We've laid aside our peaceful tasks,
We've packed out kits and gone to war.
We loved those things we left behind,
But loved our country even more.

And though we lie in some strange land,
Forgotten perhaps, by all but God
We rest in peace because we know
    Transgressors' heels shall never grind
Our country's flag into the dust.

We know, because we made it so.
The lad whose hands have milked the cow,
Whose hands have guided straight the plow;
He did not shirk his country's call,
But gladly gave his life, his all.

We loved the murmur of the brook
That flows between the mountain slopes;
The golden moon that softly smiled

As if he shared our secret hopes.

We loved the whisper of the rain
Upon the roof tops overhead;
The gleam of sun upon the snow.

We sacrificed these things we loved
To keep our flag forever free.
We know, because we made it so.

The lad whose hands made tools of steel,
Whose hands have held the big truck's wheel;
He did not shirk his country's call,
But gladly gave his life, his all.

One Little Rose

I would rather have one little rose
    From the garden of a friend
Than to have the choicest flowers
    When my stay on earth must end.

I would rather have one pleasant word
    In kindness said to me
Than flattery when my heart is still
    And life has ceased to be.
I would rather have a loving smile
    From friends I know are true
Than tears shed round by casket
    When this world I've bid adieu.

Bring me all your flowers today
    Whether pink, or white, or red;
I'd rather have one blossom now
    Than a truckload when I'm dead.

THE LADY'S A MARAUDER

The B-26 is a lady of parts,
A whole lot of trouble whenever she starts.
She's shy, she's skittish, she's coy, she's bold,
And full many a pilot she's soon turning old.

A runaway prop on the take-off, 'tis true,
Scares the hell outta me, it would out of you,
But she has them, sure, in any old season
And far's I can see, for no damn good reason.

Then she'll hold one foot daintily in air,
A cute little trick that whitens the hair.
For this baby lands at a helluva speed
And three wheels down isn't more than you need.

On the runway she crouches and waddles around
Like an old fat goose out of place on the ground.
In the air she's clean, so round and smooth,
With a little persuasion she'll fly down the groove.

When the pea-shooters threaten, she shoo's them away
Like an intent old girl too busy to play.
She doesn't hang around firing ripping bursts,
Just leaves them behind with a roaring spurt.
Of course, if they want to get rough and nasty,
She wallops them hard just for being so sassy.

"Yep," said grandpop, stroking his beard,
"I flew a twenty-six for over a year.
I wooed her and won her without much trouble,
And wherever we went, we went on the double."

And here's to the lady with the numerous quirks,
Who was always so willing to humble the squirts.
Those squirts who thought it so easy to fly.
The twenty-six flew . . . only God knows why.

     R. Burlingame
     S/Sgt, Air Corps
     22nd Bombardment Group (M)'

'This poem was discovered in the archives of the Historical Research Center, Maxwell AFB, Alabama.

xiv

From: Gerald Rasilke, 320th Bomb Group, 441st Squadron, Irving, Texas

'TWAS THE NIGHT BEFORE THE MISSION

'Twas the night before the mission
And all through the group
The Wheels and the Big Wigs
Were grinding out poop.
The bombers were parked
On their hardstands with care,
Waiting for armament
Soon to be there.
The Flyers were nestled
All snug in their beds;
While visions of milk runs
Danced in their heads.
When out of the darkness
There came a quick knock;
We cursed the O.D.
And looked at the clock.
'Briefing in two hours,'
The voice calmly said.
Well, that meant we'd have
forty more winks in bed.
Time marches on . . .
And then, yawning and sighing,
We leaped from the sack
To make with the flying.
We rush to the mess hall
Quick as a flash,
To eat powdered eggs
And hideous hash.
Then the long bumpy ride
To the Group Briefing Room,
Where the Big Wigs preside

And dish out our doom.
The target is told,
The first six rows faint,
For lo and behold,
VIENNA IT AIN'T!!
The Brain has slipped up,
My poor achin' back,
We're bombing a place
That throws up no flak!
So it's back in the truck
And off to the line;
The road is now smooth,
And the weather is fine.
The crew is at Station
The check-list is run;
The engines run smoothly
As we give 'em the gun.
Then suddenly the pilot
Calls in despair:
'Look at the Tower!
They just shot a flare!'
We dashed to the window
With heart full of dread;
The pilot was right,
The darn thing was RED!
So, it's back to the sack
And we sweat out our fate,
For there's a practice formation
At quarter past eight. ☆

Author unknown - December 1944

Our thanks to Member Bill Kearney of Dayton, Ohio, who, in WWII, served with the 739th Bomb Squadron, 454th Bomb Group, 15th Air Force, for sharing this.

Excerpts from Yank
The Army Weekly

Yank
1943 to
1945

Yank was written for the men and women in military service, the most critical audience in the World. The Army Weekly, sold only to the armed forces, captured the true feeling and spirit of Army life. In its pages, our men and women in uniform founded a new tradition in journalism.

Tight fit in a Pacific transport.—Sgt. RICHARD HANLEY

A DOGFACE ANSWERS A COLLECTION AGENCY

Pvt. Oris Turner, 39168771,
APO 000, c/o Postmaster,
San Francisco, Calif.

Dear sir:

Re: [Creditor's name]—$14.80
You have had an opportunity to settle this claim without trouble or expense, but it seems you will not settle until forced to do so. You failed even to reply to our recent letter.

Therefore, unless immediate arrangements are made for settlement, we will have no alternative but to instruct our attorneys to file a complaint against you and have you summoned to appear at the time of trial. An officer of the court will also be empowered to seize your goods, attach your earnings, automobile, bank account, or any other funds or property that may belong to you or be due you.

You would be wise to make settlement, etc., etc.
Yours,
[NAME OF COLLECTION AGENCY.]

New Guinea,
Jan. 26, 1943

Dear sirs:

Your letter of 11/19/'42 was duly rec'd today and after reading the contents therein I am pleased to note that I will be summoned to appear in court to make payment due you of $14.80 plus interest and costs.

Gentlemen, the opportunities your letter presents are beyond my wildest dreams.

I believe by law the court is required to send a process server to deliver the summons in person. In that case I will inform you of certain essentials he will require for jungle travel.

The first item advisable is a self-inflating life raft, as ships even in convoys are sometimes sunk. The raft will also be useful later in crossing rivers and swamps in New Guinea. He should also bring the following items: Mosquito bars, head net, pith helmet, quinine, salt tablets, vitamin pills, mosquito and sunburn lotions, medical supplies for tropical infections, poisonous snakes, spiders, steel helmet, gas mask, waterproof tent, heavy caliber rifle for shooting Japs, crocodiles and other game, machete, chlorine capsules, flashlight, and soap.

In choosing this process server make sure that he is not an alcoholic, as there isn't a drink to be found on the whole island. Furthermore, he must not be allergic to mosquitoes, heat rash, malaria, dengue fever, snakes, spiders, lizards, flies, crocodiles, and tall grass with a few head hunters in it. These are trivial matters and he may never come in contact with any of them, especially if his convoy is attacked by the enemy's battle fleet.

I am telling you all this as I am much concerned over his safe arrival. If he reaches this location our meeting will be much more impressive than Stanley and Livingstone's. I will see that the best possible care is taken of him on arrival. As soon as he has recovered from his jungle trip we will be on our way back to civilization and the law court. I trust he is already on his way, and I am packing my barracks bags to avoid any waste of time.

Here's hoping that this letter finds you in the best of health.

Respectfully yours,
—PVT. ORIS TURNER

A SOLDIER'S DREAM

BY SGT. BOB STUART MCKNIGHT

Scott Field, Ill.

A listless hag with a Lyster bag
  Came to me in a dream.
The listless hag rode a shiftless nag,
  The Lyster bag was green,
I don't know what was in that bag,
  What overflowed its brim;
But the listless hag had a merry jag
  And her breath was foul with gin.

The listless hag slunk off her nag
  And smiled a toothless grin.
The shiftless nag with a briskless lag
  Immersed his head in the gin.
Quite soon the shiftless nag did wag
  His tail in gruesome glee,
And the listless hag danced a teasing tag:
  Oh, what a sight to see!

The listless hag leaped on her nag
  And sailed away in the night.
The mistless moon sang a shiftless tune
  As I wept to see their flight.
I only pray some day I'll find,
  Amidst the battle's din,
A listless hag, a shiftless nag
  And a Lyster bag full of gin.

FIRST EPISTLE TO THE SELECTEES

ACCORDING TO PFC. HAROLD FLEMING

Lo, ALL ye miserable sinners, entering through the Gate of Induction *into* the Land of Khaki, hearken unto my words; for I *have* dwelt in this land for many months and mine eyes have witnessed all manner of folly and *woe*.

2 Verily have I tasted of the bitter Fruit of TS *and* drained the dregs of the Cup of Snafu:

3 Gird up thy loins, my son, and take *up* the olive drab; but act slowly and with exceeding care and hearken first to the counsel of a wiser and sadder man than thou:

4 Beware thou the Sergeant *who* is called First; he hath a pleased and foolish look but he concealeth a serpent in his heart.

5 Avoid *him* when he speaketh low and his lips smileth; he smileth not for thee; his heart rejoiceth at *the* sight of thy youth and thine ignorance.

6 He will smile and smile and work all manner of evil against thee. A wise man shuns the orderly room, but the fool *shall* dwell in the kitchen forever.

7 Unto all things there is a time: there is a time to speak and a time to be silent: be thou like unto stone in the *presence* of thy superiors, and keep thy tongue still when they shall call for volunteers.

8 The wise man searcheth out the easy details, but only a fool sticketh out *his* neck.

9 Look thou with disfavor upon the newly made corporal; he prizeth *much* his stripes and is proud and foolish; he laugheth and joketh much with the older noncoms and looketh *upon* the private with a frown.

10 He would fain go to OCS, but he is not qualified.

11 Know thou that the Sergeant of the Mess is a man of many moods: when *he* looketh pleased and his words are like honey, the wise KP seeketh him out and praiseth his chow and laugheth much at his jests:

12 But when he moveth with great haste and the sweat standeth *on* his brow *and* he *curseth* under his breath, make thyself scarce; for he will fall like a whirlwind upon the idle and the goldbrick shall know his wrath.

13 The Supply Sergeant is a lazy man *and* worketh not; but he is the keeper of many good things: if thou wouldst wear well-fitting raiment and avoid the statement of charges, *make* him thy friend.

14 He prizeth drunkenness *above* all things.

15 He careth not for praise or flattery, but lend him *thy* lucre and thy liquor and he will love thee.

16 Hell hath no fury like a Shavetail scorned: he walketh with a swagger and regardeth the enlisted man with a raised eyebrow; he looketh upon his bars with exceeding pleasure *and* loveth a salute mightily.

17 Act thou lowly unto him and call him sir and he will love thee.

18 Damned *be* he who standeth first in the line of chow and shortstoppeth the dessert and cincheth the coffee.

19 He taketh from the meat dish with a heavy hand and leaveth thee the bony *part*.

20 He is thrice cursed, and all *people*, even unto the pfcs, will revile him and spit upon him: *for* his name is called Chow Hound, and he is an abomination.

21 Know thou the Big Operator, but trust him not: he *worketh* always upon a deal and he speaketh confidentially.

22 He knoweth many women and goeth into town every night; he borroweth all thy money; yea, even *unto* thy ration check.

23 He promiseth to fix thee up, but doth *it* not.

24 Beware thou the Old Man, for he will make *thee* sweat; when he approacheth, look thou on the ball; he loveth to chew upon thy posterior.

25 Keep thou out of his sight and let him not *know* thee by name: for he who arouseth the wrath of the Old Man shall *go* many times unto the chaplain. *Selah*.

"It's from the old man. He says we're due for typhoid booster shots."—*Cpl. Fred Schwab.*

FALL OUT FOR AN INTERVIEW

By Sgt. RAY DUNCAN

I'M KEEPING a scrapbook of newspaper stories about movie stars in the service. I suppose the rest of you soldiers are doing the same thing. If you can bear to part with any of your clippings about Hollywood men in uniform, I certainly would like to buy them from you. Or maybe we could trade duplicates.

The newspapers are doing an excellent job of covering film actor-soldiers. Only trouble with this kind of reporting is that there's not enough of it. It would be nice if similar stories could be done about all of our servicemen.

Surely there are enough good writers in this country to cover the activities of every GI in full glamorous detail.

Take for instance Floyd Pringle. He used to be pin boy at the Sportland Bowling Alley in Little Ditch, Ohio. When Floyd was drafted there should have been a story like this in all the papers:

LITTLE DITCH, OHIO, Feb. 21—He used to set 'em up for the Sportland bowlers—now he'll mow 'em down for the United Nations!

Into the greatest match of his career today went pale, slender Floyd Pringle. The idol of thousands of Little Ditch bowlers joined the United States Army!

Grinning happily as he reported for induction, Pringle appeared pleased when informed that he had been selected for 13 weeks of basic training.

The famed pin boy did not apply for a commission. He stated simply that he wished to serve in the ranks with the ordinary soldiers.

Flashing the famous Pringle grin that thrilled thousands in Little Ditch, he said: "Anybody who can dodge bowling balls can dodge Nazi bullets!"

Floyd Pringle awaited his turn in line at the induction station, just like everyone else. Everybody said he was a "regular guy" and a "swell fellow," and the examining doctor declared he was a "splendid physical specimen."

Think of the boost to Army morale if every GI hit the metropolitan press with a story like that!

Now suppose that our hero comes home on furlough from foreign service. Still following the model of the write-ups about the movie stars, the press would flash a story like this over the wires:

LITTLE DITCH, OHIO, Dec. 19—Back from the battle front today came Pvt. Floyd Pringle, his face drawn and a little haggard beneath its rich overseas tan.

The celebrated pin boy from this tiny Ohio town has been on a dangerous ammunition-supply mission in a combat zone, the nature of which cannot be disclosed.

(This is an example of tactful handling of mate-

rial by a skillful newspaper writer. What Floyd actually told reporters was this: "I am a basic in a gun crew and I have to carry the shells from the truck and make a pile on the ground. We never saw no action. We had a dry run every day, and the rest of the time we set on our dead hams." . . . Now go on with the news story.)

Pvt. Pringle received an ovation when he arrived at the Little Ditch station. Women on the street stared at him in frank admiration, and several girls made low whistling noises.

The Pringle charm, which brightened Sportland alleys for so long, has not been dimmed by the strenuous army training which Pringle endured without complaint.

Pringle has been on a dangerous combat mission in a war zone. He goes on all the marches with the men in his crew and insists on sharing every hardship equally with the others.

Reports from the fighting front are that Pvt. Floyd Pringle is a "swell fellow" and a "regular guy," just as common and unaffected as any man in the dangerous combat war zone.

Remember, a glamorous soldier is a good soldier. Why be content with your name on a billboard honor roll in a vacant lot? Why not sit down right now and cut a stencil, to be run off and mailed to every editor in the land, urging the full glamor treatment for all of our boys in the service?

"I'd like a little fatherly advice, Sir."—Cpl. Ernest Maxwell

A SACK OF MAIL

By Cpl. PAUL E. DEUTSCHMANN

Sketch by Sgt. Frank Brandt

SOMEWHERE IN SARDINIA—Mail call is one of the most important things in a GI's life, I was reading the other day. It's good for that ethereal something that USO hostesses, advertising copywriters and sundry other civilians back home call morale. With the correspondents some GIs have, though, no mail is good mail. Leave us look at some of these morale-boosters.

FIDGETY-FILLY TYPE

"Snookie, dear—I drove out to Petter's Perch the other night, along the Old Mill Road. You remember, don't you, dear? The moon was bright and the stars twinkled just like when you were there with me, and it made me feel so-o-o romantic!

"Some girls complain about the man shortage. But not me! Last night three fellows took me to the movies, and afterwards they took turns with me out on the back porch—dancing. But don't worry, dear, they were all servicemen. I won't go out with a man except in uniform. One of them, Casper Clutchem, who is sorta blond and cute and a Marine sergeant, says for me to tell you 'the situation is under control.' He is *awful* strong.

"Guess what we were drinking? Those potent daiquiris. They really make me forget myself—almost.

"And, did I tell you? Casper is stationed just outside of town and has promised to come see me real often. I couldn't very well refuse him because he said he was leaving for overseas almost any month now. I believe in doing my bit to help the servicemen because, after all, some of them are so far from home and don't know a soul in town."

HOME-GUARD TYPE

"Dear Corp—I am back in Dayton for another furlough and I am looking after Lulu, just like you asked me to. She's really a wonderful gal and a smooth dancer. And if she weren't your wife I could really go for her myself. Do you realize, I've gotten to know Lulu better than you do—almost! And boy, can she hold her likker!

"We had dinner at the Cove tonight and are now back at your apartment. It is just midnight, and while Lulu is slipping into something more *comfortable*, I thought I'd drop you a line. Ha ha, old man, I'm only kidding."

MAN-OF-AFFAIRS TYPE

"I've been doing swell at the office. Just got the Whatsis Soap and Whoozis Hosiery account. That's $4,000,000 billing besides the pleasure I get from interviewing models for the 'leg art' pictures. But it's nothing like the swell job you boys are doing over there. I wish I were in there with you, but——

"Give 'em hell for me, old fellow! They asked for it—and we're just the guys to give it to them. I'm buying War Bonds like an insane stamp collector. I really wish I were out in the foxholes with you, but——"

CIVILIAN BRASS-HAT TYPE

"Dear Bill—All of us here at the Old Company, from the office staff up to me, are thinking of you boys in the service and doing our part to help you fellas. We're all buying War Bonds and cutting down on meat and butter—and some of the girls in the office are even rolling bandages on Saturday afternoons, when they aren't working.

"Rationing is pretty grim now. Steaks only twice a week and no more cherries in cherry cokes. But we don't mind because the papers say that you fellows overseas are getting all the good things—and you certainly deserve them.

"Yes sir, no one can say that the Old Company is not well represented in the foxholes and trenches of our fighting fronts all over the globe. Rollie is a warrant officer at Camp Dix, N. J., and Jim is at the Brooklyn Navy Yard, and Harry is a chauffeur to a Marine colonel in Philadelphia. Van is way down in Texas and Charlie is a quartermaster clerk in Georgia and you're in the Infantry in Italy. Give 'em hell, boy."

OH-YOU-DEVIL TYPE

"You guys over there in Italy must be having a big time with all those little dark-eyed signorinas. Do they wear those grass skirts like Dorothy Lamour?"

LOCAL-BOY-MAKES-GOOD TYPE

"Your cousin Herman is now a technical sergeant and he has only been in the Army five months. I can't understand why you're still a corporal. Are your officers mad at you?"

ALL-IN-THIS-TOGETHER TYPE

"Dear Pal—Things are really getting rugged now at good old Camp Kilmer. I can only get off every other week end. We went out on bivouac last week and, boy, was it rough! We slept in pup tents for three nights—right on the ground.

"Last week I was awarded the Good Conduct Ribbon at a special ceremony. You might not hear from me for a while, as I am expecting to be shipped out any day now—to North Carolina.

"By the way—what is this Spam we hear so much about?"

THE LEGION OF THE UNCOUTH

BY S/SGT. THOMAS P. ASHLOCK

Australia

The pages of the magazines back home
That feature stuff of war—the march of men,
The awesome crawl of tanks, the flight of planes—
Have shown a tiresome lot of "glamor Yanks,"
With trousers razor-creased and shirts that still
Retain the sheen of new-spun factory cloth;
With ties adjusted right, and shoes, the gleam
Of which will blind. Too much of new-blown rank,
With chevrons bright and neatly sewn on sleeves
Of sarge or corp; and when I view those lads,
So sartorially complete and nice, I think
Of Hollywood, with extras dressed to fit
A part in some stage scene, instead of soldiers
Girt for deadly, bloody, filthy war.

From the Stevens in Chicago town,
To our sun-blistered, bug-infested post,
Is a far, unholy cry—and the difference
Much the same as that which lies between
My lady's boudoir and a stable stall:
For here we boys are not—oh, really not
The photogenic type! Our hair grows long,
We seldom shave; Svengali would be proud

To flaunt the beards that some of us have grown.
Our pants are frayed and bleached and baggy-kneed;
We wear no shirts—and as for ties,—say, tell
Us, please—what is a tie?
And it's a certain sign
You're "tropo," if you start to shine your shoes!

We're a motley, rugged, crumby lot,
No subjects for a Sunday supplement:
But somehow, I don't think a man of us,
Deep down within his heart, would trade his place
With fortune's darlings in the Stevens lounge.
We're "in" the thing, you see—not quite as much
But something like—our buddies at Bataan,
Corregidor, the Solomons, and Wake;
And because we walk in shabbiness—unkempt,
Ungroomed—and live with pests, and breathe red dust
And thirst and bake in searing heat, and drown
In tropic rains,—like them—we're fiercely proud.
Let others have the dress parade, the show,
The full-page spread in magazines. We like
Our role—the real, the earnest, cussin' sweatin'
Dirty, ugly role of men *at* war!

LULLABY

BY SGT. CHARLES E. BUTLER (*Britain*)

For a photograph with the caption: "Here are three American soldiers who were killed in battle on the beach at Buna, New Guinea. This photograph, emphasizing the grim facts of war, was released to give the American public a more realistic picture of the war."

Was it evening, with a slow wind falling
Upon the gray and broken stillness in the leaves,
The birds calling in terror, and the sky
Broken with wings, and on the drifting shore
The slow tide curling inward, curving and rippling,
Fold upon foam-edged fold, folding at last
Upon you in the sand? Was it evening then,
And quiet, falling to sleep in the silence,
You, with your cheek soft on the ultimate pillow
And your outstretched hand reaching no more for the
   gun,
Or love, or the things of life, sleeping there, sleeping?

You have come a long way to lie on the sand,
Forgetful of the motion of
The slow, incessant waves
Curving and falling, the white foam lifting
The white sand drifting
Over your face, your outflung hand,
Drifting and creeping
Slow and incessant and cool . . . .
You have come a long way, a world away, to sleep.

The page will remember a little while;
You are a warning now; a message,
Sleeping like children on the rippled shore,
Forgetful now for ever of the slow
Whispers of the curling water
Sifting the sand around you with its long
Reiterant falling and lifting whispering music . . .
You are a message now, forgetful, sleeping;
The idiot print of Time on the wave-washed shore . . .

Sleep now, forgetful of the drifting sand,
The strange cries of birds in the green forest;
Sleep, cold on the sand, immortal on the fading page,
Emphatic, grim, forgetful . . . Sleep, sleep . . .
Silence will shield the shrieking of the birds,
The wild, quick beating of their wings against the tree
   fronds;
The storm will pass . . . Silence will cover it;
Sleep . . .

MAIL CALL

DEEP IN THE HEART

DEAR YANK:

Recently I was a dinner guest of the president of the Texas Christian Federation of Women's Clubs in Brownwood, Tex. The hostess told me she had tried to get her club to invite soldiers to members' homes, and I thought GIs would like to see the reply she got from one of the members. Unfortunately it is representative of what the "better class" of moguls really think. Here's the letter:

Dear Mrs. President. When you propose that we ask soldiers to our homes we feel as though you have failed us in the most critical situation which has ever arisen to face us. To ask the women of Texas to place their daughters on the altar of sacrifice to the evil that will come from the program which you presented is asking too much. I know our boys are lonely, but unless they have manhood enough to deny themselves some things for a few short months I do not believe they are courageous enough to sustain our democratic government.

Let us just look at the situation. If the social contacts at the camps were the end of those meetings quite another outlook could be seen, but you know those boys will go out on the week ends and contact our girls again. This time they will not be chaperoned, and for the virtue of how many girls who have thus lost their purity will we be held accountable? We just can't do this. Do not let us sell our daughters in such a racket. Maybe a few would meet life companions, but think of the sorrow and misery and sin we would be leading the numberless ones into! Men and women of the convention were hurt by your proposal. The decision almost wholly was that we mothers and fathers will not stand for this. We feel that the class of boys whom the girls would meet under your plan are the ones who deliberately want to meet strange girls and they are not the best class of selectees. Many are filled with uncontrolled passion and lust, and many of them are married. I am willing to sacrifice my time, my money and all my material profits for my country, but I cannot give my daughter in such a useless cause.

Well, I just thought you'd like to know what to expect when this melee is over.

Camp Bowie, Tex. —PFC. JAMES L. SCOTT

DEAR YANK:

I have never wanted to be quoted publicly before, and this is the first time I have ever written to any publication, but this is also the first time I have ever been so burned up. As a native Texan, and mighty proud of it, I found the letter submitted by a Camp Bowie (Tex.) soldier, which had been written by a member of the Texas Christian Federation of Women's Clubs in Brownwood, Tex., the most disgusting piece of writing I have ever had the misfortune to read. It is certainly the least representative of any I have ever read about Texas women. . . . Brother, she is no real Texan.

On Maneuvers —LT. H. H. MONTGOMERY

DEAR YANK:

. . . . She very plainly shows that she herself does not have any knowledge of the term "our democratic government," of which she speaks. . . . This woman has certainly made a bad impression of herself, her club and the state of Texas as a whole. . . .

Panama —PVT. ELWOOD J. HALE

DEAR YANK:

. . . Any girl who would have relations with a fellow under the conditions proposed by the woman in Texas is not the type coming up to my level and caliber. That, I believe, speaks for the entire personnel of the armed services of our country.

Antigua —PFC. WILLIAM D. TAYLOR

DEAR YANK:

. . . And that remark about Deep in the Heart. We're proud of who wrote it, as we want our gals as we left them and we don't want them on the altar of sacrifice. We are glad the mothers of Texas are holding on to their daughters and that they hold their respect.

Attu —SGT. DELMOS DANIELS

DEAR YANK:

"I am willing to sacrifice my time, my money, and all my material profits for my country, but I cannot give my daughter. . . ." This is from that letter quoted in YANK. To it I add a poem:

THE ULTIMATE SACRIFICE

My daughter is precious; she's finer than gold,
But hardly constructed for soldiers to hold.
    A soldier's the sort
    For rapine and slaughter,
    Not fit to escort
    A patriot's daughter.
I'll sacrifice time, but dear me! I falter
When requested to lay my poor girl on the altar.

I know that the men must be awfully lonely;
I'd like to assist them if possible, only
    The boys may be tempted
    To ask for a date;
    No girl is exempted
    When staying out late
From possible harm by inordinate passion
And a plunge into ruin in the most expedite fashion.

Beware of the soldier who comes to your house;
It's a hundred to one he's a wolf or a louse.
    You will certainly find,
    If you scratch a GI,
    A lecherous mind
    And a wandering eye.
The soldier who enters your home's of a surety
An imminent threat to your daughter's security.

Camp Shelby, Miss. —S/SGT. GRANT A. SANDERS

DEAR YANK:

. . . . The remark about selling daughters to American soldiers is one of the most stupid remarks any normal person has ever made. . . .

India —S/SGT. JOHN GRIDER °

° *Also signed by Pvt. Peter Manquacine.*

A soldier of the Shamrock Battalion moves up on Makin. —Sgt. JOHN BUSHEMI

DEAR YANK:

. . . I have never known of a Christian person with such a nasty and inconsiderate attitude toward the men and boys that are serving their country in these trying times. Any girl that has to have a chaperon along on a date to remain pure and clean is not the type of girl that a soldier would like to be seen in public with. . . .

Hawaii —PVT. DORSEY WIGGINS °

° *Also signed by Sgt. Lester, T-5s Howell, Rouse and Wilkinson and Pfc. Lemmens.*

DEAR YANK:

YANK acted in good faith in publishing Pfc. James Scott's letter in regard to the feelings of the mothers of Brownwood—it was James Scott who acted in ill faith in submitting a letter without explaining the circumstances surrounding the letter. . . . [It] was written over three years ago by a woman who lived approximately 150 miles southwest of Brownwood and who, at that time, had probably not met a single one of our new brand of GIs. It was written to a woman who lived in Austin, Tex. A copy of that letter was sent to a Brownwood woman because it was outrageously dramatic enough to be funny. . . .

—MUZELLE STANLEY
Brownwood, Tex.   City Recreation Supervisor

MERCY FOR JAPS

DEAR YANK:

As God is my witness I am sorry to read of the way two American soldiers treated the enemy on Makin Island; they shot some Japanese when they might have been able to take them alive. I don't believe in killing unless it has to be done. I am a servant of God, so when I get into battle I hope by His help to take as many Japs alive as I can. If I am compelled to destroy lives in battle I shall do so, but when U. S. troops throw grenades into an enemy position and Japs run out unarmed we should make an effort to take them alive. I know that if I were in a dugout and forced to run out I would want mercy.

Camp Davis, N. C. —PVT. RALPH H. LUCKEY

DEAR YANK:

We just read the letter written by that servant of God, Pvt. Luckey, and wish to state that he has the wrong slant. . . . After being in combat and seeing medics being killed trying to help our wounded makes you want to kill the bastards. . . . Fair play is fine among sportsmen but we are fighting back stabbers! . . .

Hawaii Jap Killers °

° *Signed by Pvt. P. Stupar.*

DEAR YANK:

. . . NO MERCY FOR MURDERERS!

On Maneuvers —PVT. SAM BONANNO

DEAR YANK:

Brother, Pvt. Luckey better live up to his last name if he goes into combat with the idea of taking Jap prisoners alive!

Port of Embarkation —SGT. CARL BETHEA °

° *Also signed by 13 others.*

DEAR YANK:

We are all Navy men who are suffering from combat fatigue. Many of us have been strafed by Jap Zeros while floating helplessly in the sea and have seen what the soldiers and marines have gone through in this fight. If Pvt. Luckey heeds his own call for mercy for Japs, his soul will belong to God but his body will belong to the Japs. . . .

—VETS OF WORLD WAR II
Norfolk Naval Hosp., Portsmouth, Va.

DEAR YANK:

. . . If I had another chance I certainly would do the the same thing those Yanks on Makin did. Shoot 'em and shoot 'em dead. I know what I'm talking about. I have been there.

Camp Blanding, Fla. —T/SGT. J. N. OLSEN

DEAR YANK:

. . . Please notify the FBI, G-2, anything—but have that guy locked up!

Fort Custer, Mich. —CPL. S. SCHWARTZ

DEAR YANK:

Has Pvt. Luckey ever seen his friends and buddies shot down by the Japs? Has he ever carried our dead out of the jungle for burial? I have—and more, during the eight months I spent on Guadalcanal. Pvt. Luckey will have no dead Japs on his conscience when they kill him.

—PVT. C. E. CARTER
Harmon Gen. Hosp., Longview, Tex.

DEAR YANK:

. . . Luckey is out of this world and should be confined in a small room heavily padded on four sides.

Bermuda —S/SGT. ARTHUR J. KAPLAN

DEAR YANK:

Me and my buddies sure were mad as hell when we read Pvt. Ralph Luckey's letter. He sure shot off his mouth about our treatment of the Japs. The trouble is that he has had it nice and soft so far. . . .

Trinidad —PFC. EDWARD STAFFIN

DEAR YANK:

. . . We don't know whether to feel sorry for this guy or just laugh the thing off. . . .

—M/SGT. W. F. HARDGROVE °
NC Hosp., Mitchel Field, N. Y. (South Pacific)

° *Signed also by M/Sgt. R. M. Stephens (SWP); T/Sgts. L. C. Sheehan (Britain) and N. Sedorick (Britain); S/Sgts. P. F. Teraberry (Italy, Africa), R. I. Vogel (Italy, Africa), L. V. Behout (CBI), J. M. Haresign (Italy) and H. R. Garrison (New Guinea); Sgts. W. J. Polera, P. Nadzak (CBI) and J. Seginah (Britain), and Cpl. M. J. Bursie (New Guinea).*

DEAR YANK:

. . . Wake up, Luckey. The Jap doesn't care if God is his witness or not.

—PFC. CHARLES J. NICHOLS
Worthington Gen. Hosp., Tuscaloosa, Ala.

DEAR YANK:

It's evening. We're sitting about two feet from our foxhole thinking about a letter written by Pvt. Ralph H. Luckey from Camp Davis, N. C. in a recent issue of YANK. Do you mind if we ask him a question? Pvt.

Luckey, you're now living in an Army camp, just as we did. Making friends, just as we did. Friends who, in time, will be much closer, dearer, to you than you would believe possible.

We bunked together, ate together, laughed and played together, worked and dated together. Recently we fought together. During the battle, Blackie was wounded and taken prisoner. When we advanced several hours later, we found Blackie. His cheeks were punctured by sharp sticks—pulled tight by a wire tourniquet, the sticks acting as a bit does for a horse's mouth. There were slits made by a knife along the center of his legs and on his side—just as if an artist had taken pride in an act of torture well done.

We continued to move on. Do you think that we also continued to remember the niceties of civilized warfare?

Central Pacific   —s/SGT. B. W. MILEWSKI

This is the last of a series of GI comments in reply to Pvt. Luckey's letter. YANK has received a great number of letters on the subject, but only two readers supported the point of view advocated by Pvt. Luckey.

THANKS

DEAR YANK:

I would like to express my thanks to some unknown GI who looked after my mother when she wasn't feeling well on a train trip from Illinois to California this past December. Perhaps I can return the favor some day, soldier.

The Aleutians   —PFC. B. FELDMAN

A COLONEL SPEAKS

DEAR YANK:

Allow me, a low-serial-number Regular Army colonel, to add to the gripe of Pvt. David W. Wallace [who complained that "practically every café fit to patronize in Cairo, Egypt, is out of bounds to American enlisted men."—Ed.] It griped me, too, when in Cairo, to see privately owned, operated-for-profit night clubs open to all the public *except* GIs. Not only that, but with military police at the door to keep out the "untouchables."

Well, Wallace, let me describe what you were missing. Club No. 1 on my list: Infested ·with greasy looking Levantines of indeterminate origin accompanied by their high-priced "companions." Tom Collins quite expensive, made up of lukewarm Orange Crush and poor gin. . . . A helluva big check after a not very thrilling evening. Club No. 2: Fairly nice crowd except for one fat civilian surrounded by some hard-looking tarts on the make. He was trying rather unsuccessfully to get some young officers over to his table. Floor show lousy —belly dancers couldn't get even a trial on a Minsky circuit. Food fair, but "extras" very expensive. Officers there looked as if they wouldn't mind rubbing shoulders with other ranks.

No, soldier, you didn't miss much.

Just the same, I didn't like the signs "Military Personnel—Officers Only" one bit. One American GI is worth a helluva lot more than the best of the civilians I saw at those night clubs I attended. And from what I saw of our enlisted men in Cairo they would, by their neatness, general gentlemanly conduct and military

bearing, be an asset to any of the privately owned open-to-the-public clubs I've ever seen anywhere.

I hope the situation in Cairo changes under new management.

Italy   —An Officer and American Soldier

MONOTONY

DEAR YANK:

Monotony, monotony, all is monotony. The heat, the insects, the work, the complete absence of towns, women, liquor. Every too often the incredible routine inspection for diseases which couldn't possibly be there, under the circumstances. The irregular mail, which has become regular in its irregularity. The pay ritual; the eagle screams and so does the local GI, who has no choice but to send the money home—a prudent but singularly unsatisfying action. On a more personal basis, the monotony of prefixing the name with those three little —awfully little—letters: pfc.

All this monotony, and more, existed before. Then came the brilliant idea of subscribing to YANK. It all seemed so simple at the time. "Just send us your money order for two bucks," you said, "and before you know it YANK will be coming around regularly to cheer your spirit and brighten your days." So I did it. I sent the money order for two bucks. And what happened? I found that I had added a new monotony to the existing ones. With dreary, weary regularity I found myself writing letters to YANK on a regular basis, always dealing with the same topic: Where is the magazine? With equally monotonous regularity did I get no answer. Fellers, enough is enough. The heat, the insects, the lack of diversion—all these things you can do nothing about. But this one-sided correspondence. . . . Write to me, huh? Better yet, if you can possibly see your way clear, send me the damn magazine!

New Hebrides   —PFC. H. MOLDAUER

So *that's* where that two bucks came from.

PRAISE FOR MEDICS

DEAR YANK:

We have been and still are in combat and have decided to spend a little time in order to let you know about some real fighting men. They are the first-aid men in the Medics. They are doing a wonderful job here in the front lines. We infantrymen here take our hats off to them and would like to see them get a little more credit and praise.

Italy   —PVT. JOE MC GUIRE °

° *Also signed by Pfc. E. Charon.*

DEMOCRACY?

DEAR YANK:

Here is a question that each Negro soldier is asking. What is the Negro soldier fighting for? On whose team are we playing? Myself and eight other soldiers were on our way from Camp Claiborne, La., to the hospital here at Fort Huachuca. We had to lay over until the next day for our train. On the next day we could not purchase a cup of coffee at any of the lunchrooms around there. As you know, Old Man Jim Crow rules. The only

This wave has just hit the beach at Eniwetok in the Marshalls.—Sgt. JOHN BUSHEMI

In liberated Rome a Yank holds an Italian baby.—Sgt. GEORGE AARONS

place where we could be served was at the lunchroom at the railroad station but, of course, we had to go into the kitchen. But that's not all; 11:30 A.M. about two dozen German prisoners of war, with two American guards, came to the station. They entered the lunchroom, sat at the tables, had their meals served, talked, smoked, in fact had quite a swell time. I stood on the outside looking on, and I could not help but ask myself these questions: Are these men sworn enemies of this country? Are they not taught to hate and destroy . . . all democratic governments? Are we not American soldiers, sworn to fight for and die if need be for this our country? Then why are they treated better than we are? Why are we pushed around like cattle? If we are fighting for the same thing, if we are to die for our country, then why does the Government allow such things to go on? Some of the boys are saying that you will not print this letter. I'm saying that you will. . . .

Fort Huachuca, Ariz.   —CPL. RUPERT TRIMMINGHAM

DEAR YANK:

I am writing to you in regard to the incident told in a letter to you by Cpl. Trimmingham (Negro) describing the way he was forced to eat in the kitchen of a station restaurant while a group of German prisoners were fed with the rest of the white civilians in the restaurant. Gentlemen, I am a Southern rebel, but this incident makes me none the more proud of my Southern heritage! Frankly, I think that this incident is a disgrace to a democratic nation such as ours is supposed to be. Are we fighting for such a thing as this? Certainly not. If this incident is democracy, I don't want any part of it! . . . I wonder what the "Aryan supermen" think when they get a first-hand glimpse of our racial discrimination. Are we not waging a war, in part, for this fundamental of democracy? In closing, let me say that a lot of us, especially in the South, should cast the beam out of our own eyes before we try to do so in others, across the seas.

—CPL. HENRY S. WOOTTON JR. *

Fairfield-Suisun AAF, Calif.

* Also signed by S/Sgt. A. S. Tepper and Pfc. Jose Rosenzweig.*

DEAR YANK:

You are to be complimented on having the courage to print Cpl. Trimmingham's letter in an April issue of YANK. It simply proves that your policy is maturing editorially. He [Cpl. Trimmingham] probes an old wound when he exposes the problem of our colored soldiers throughout the South. It seems incredible that German prisoners of war should be afforded the amenities while our own men—in uniform and changing stations—are denied similar attention because of color and the vicious attitude of certain portions of our country. What sort of a deal is this? It is, I think, high time that this festering sore was cut out by intelligent social surgeons once and for all. I can well understand and sympathize with the corporal's implied but unwritten question: why, then are we in uniform. Has it occurred to anyone that those Boche prisoners of war must be still laughing at us?

Bermuda   —S/SGT. ARTHUR J. KAPLAN

DEAR YANK:

. . . I'm not a Negro, but I've been around and know what the score is. I want to thank the YANK . . . and congratulate Cpl. Rupert Trimmingham.

Port of Embarkation   —PVT. GUSTAVE SANTIAGO

DEAR YANK:

Just read Cpl. Rupert Trimmingham's letter titled "Democracy?" in an April edition of YANK. We are white soldiers in the Burma jungles, and there are many Negro outfits working with us. They are doing more than their part to win this war. We are proud of the colored men here. When we are away from camp working in the jungles, we can go to any colored camp and be treated like one of their own. I think it is a disgrace that, while we are away from home doing our part to help win the war, some people back home are knocking down everything that we are fighting for.

We are among many Allied Nations' soldiers that are fighting here, and they marvel at how the American Army, which is composed of so many nationalities and different races, gets along so well. We are ashamed to read that the German soldier, who is the sworn enemy of our country, is treated better than the soldier of our country, because of race.

Cpl. Trimmingham asked: What is a Negro fighting for? If this sort of thing continues, we the white soldiers will begin to wonder: What are *we* fighting for?

Burma   —PVT. JOSEPH POSCUCCI (Italian) *

* Also signed by Cpl. Edward A. Kreutler (French), Pfc. Maurice E. Wenson (Swedish) and Pvt. James F. Malloy (Irish).*

DEAR YANK:

Allow me to thank you for publishing my letter. Although there was some doubt about its being published, yet somehow I felt that YANK was too great a paper not to. . . . Each day brings three, four or five letters to me in answer to my letter. I just returned from my furlough and found 25 letters awaiting me. To date I've received 287 letters, and, strange as it may seem, 183 are from white men and women in the armed service. Another strange feature about these letters is that the most of these people are from the Deep South. They are all proud of the fact that they are of the South but ashamed to learn that there are so many of their own people who by their actions and manner toward the Negro are playing Hitler's game. Nevertheless, it gives me new hope to realize that there are doubtless thousands of whites who are willing to fight this Frankenstein that so many white people are keeping alive. All that the Negro is asking for is to be given half a chance and he will soon demonstrate his worth to his country. Should these white people who realize that the Negro is a man who is loyal—one who would gladly give his life for this our wonderful country—would stand up, join with us and help us to prove to their white friends that we are worthy, I'm sure that we would bury race hate and unfair treatment. Thanks again.

Fort Huachuca, Ariz.   —CPL. RUPERT TRIMMINGHAM

Since YANK printed Cpl. Trimmingham's letter we have received a great number of comments from GIs, almost all of whom were outraged by the treatment given the corporal. His letter has been taken from YANK and widely quoted. The incident has been dramatized on the air and was the basis for a moving short story published recently in the *New Yorker* magazine.

PIN-UPS

DEAR YANK:

We boys do not approve of your very indecent portrayal of the spicy looking female in a recent edition of our much-loved and eagerly read YANK. It seems the intelligent-looking Irene Manning would never pose for such a suggestive-looking picture. We may seem old-fashioned, but sending YANK home to wives and sweethearts with such a seductive-looking picture, we feel compelled to make an apology for this issue.

Is this the much publicized "Pin-Up Girl" that the Yankee soldiers so crave? We have our doubts! Miss Manning is well dressed, but the pose—phew! (Hays office please take note.)

Believe it or not, our average age is 23.
Britain —SGT. E. W. O'HARA °

° *Also signed by Cpl. P. Pistocco Jr. and D. E. Clark.*

DEAR YANK:

I don't know who started this idea of pin-ups, but they say that it is supposed to help keep up the morale of the servicemen, or something like that. Here is my idea of the help it is. In the first place, I would say that 24 out of 25 of the men in the service are either married or have a girl at home whom they respect and intend to marry as soon as this war is over. . . . How many of you GIs would like to go home and find the room of your wife or girl friend covered with pictures of a guy stepping out of a bathtub, draped only in a skimpy little towel, or see the walls covered with the pictures of a shorts advertisement or such pictures? None of you would. Then why keep a lot of junk hanging around and kid yourself about keeping up morale? . . .

I would much rather wake up in the morning and see a picture of a P-51 or 39 hanging above my bed or over the picture of my wife, whom I think is the best-looking girl in the world, than of some dame who has been kidded into or highly paid for posing for these pictures.
Myrtle Beach AAF, S. C. —PFC. JOSEPH H. SALING

DEAR YANK:

Sgt. E. W. O'Hara, in a recent letter about pin-ups in YANK, speaks of "suggestiveness" in the "seductive-looking" picture of Miss Irene Manning. For the life of me, I can't see anything suggestive about it. Shouldn't you say that the suggestiveness and the suggestive look come from an "unclean" mind, not from the picture? . . .
Panama —S/SGT. CLIFF CROUCH °

° *Also signed by S/Sgt. Raymond Cox.*

DEAR YANK:

. . . Don't slam our pin-ups. If I had a wife I would make sure her picture was up, but Irene Manning will do until that big day.
Fleet Post Office —S1C. R. C. WALTERS

DEAR YANK:

. . . Maybe if some of those panty-waists had to be stuck out some place where there were no white women and few native women for a year and a half, as we were, they would appreciate even a picture of our gals back home. The good sergeant [and the other two signers of his letter] alibi that perhaps they are old-fashioned and go so far as to apologize for the mag [when

sending it home]. . . . They must be dead from the neck up—and down. They can take their apology and jam it and cram it. And Pfc. Joseph H. Saling isn't he just too too? We suggest that when the next issue of YANK hits the PX these little boys refrain from buying it, as it is too rugged a mag for them to be reading. Perhaps later, when they grow up. We nasty old Engineers still appreciate YANK *with* its pin-ups.
Alaska —T-5 CHET STRAIGHT °

° *Also signed by T-5s F. A. Wallbaum and Cooper Dunn and Pfcs. Robert Ross, Lloyd W. Finley and Elom Calden.*

DEAR YANK:

. . . I can't understand why you would even publish such a letter. In my opinion Sgt. O'Hara owes Miss Manning an apology for his rude description of her picture. I have that picture over my locker and like it very much. I suggest Sgt. O'Hara go out and learn the facts of life from someone who has been around. Also, the boys in my platoon agree with me that he should be examined for Sec. 8. Keep the pin-up pictures coming. We like them.
Camp McCain, Miss. —CPL. JOHN R. CREICH

DEAR YANK:

Why we GIs over here in the Pacific have to read your tripe and drivel about the Wacs beats me. Who in the hell cares about these dimpled GIs who are supposed to be soldiers? All I have ever heard of them doing is peeling spuds, clerking in the office, driving a truck or tractor or puttering around in a photo lab. Yet all the stories written about our dears tell how over-worked they are. I correspond regularly with a close relative of mine who is a Wac, and all she writes about is the dances, picnics, swimming parties and bars she has attended. Are these janes in the Army for the same reasons we are, or just to see how many dates they can get? We would like them a hell of a lot better, and respect them more, if they did their part in some defense plant or at home, where they belong. So please let up on the cock and bull and feminine propaganda. It's sickening to read about some doll who has made the supreme sacrifice of giving up her lace-trimmed undies for ODs.
New Hebrides —SGT. BOB BOWIE

DEAR YANK:

I was disgusted when I opened the pages of a recent YANK and saw some silly female in GI clothes. I detest the Wacs very thoroughly and I hope I never meet one. That is also the opinion of all my buddies.
New Zealand —PVT. WILLIAM J. ROBINSON

WACS HIT BACK

DEAR YANK:

After reading the letters of Sgt. Bob Bowie and Pvt. William Robinson [in a February issue] I think it is about time the Wacs had their say. Their stubborn, prejudiced attitude makes many of us wonder if it is really worth it all. . . . There are many heartbreaking stories behind many of our enlistees, stories that have not been published and will never be known, and there is a wealth of patriotism and sincere motives to be found in these girls.
Fort Crook, Nebr. —PVT. CAROL J. SWAN

ROSIE'S RIVETERS

BY SGT. SAUL LEVITT

Rosie poses for a picture at his home base in England with some of the men who have sweated out
many missions over Europe in his veteran Fortress.

Front (l. to r.): Lt. R. C. Bailey, Capt. R. Rosenthal, Lt. C. J. Milburn and Lt. W. T. Lewis. Back row (l. to r.): S/Sgt. L. F. Darling, T/Sgt. M. V. Bocuzzi, S/Sgt. J. F. Mack, T/Sgt. C. C. Hall, S/Sgt. W. J. DeBlasio and S/Sgt. R. H. Robinson.

ENGLAND—For newspapers, bigger victories in this war are a simple problem—you just use bigger type on page one. Like the American daylights raids on Berlin. In somebody's 20-volume history of the second World War, to be written in 1955, an aging crew chief like J. E. Woodard and a tail-gunner like Bill DeBlasio will find the Berlin raids rating a paragraph or two on page 963. For the men concerned with them only yesterday, they meant another evening return of tired, living men—or another ship sloping down to the limbo of "missing in action."

Sometimes even a working airfield gets a sense of something special and enormous. On one field the crews had this feeling about the Berlin raids, when a certain plane came swinging low over the tower, home from Berlin, one late afternoon.

The plane was Capt. Robert Rosenthal's—*Rosie's Riveters*. Her crew came home to a sudden, unrestrained, crazy holiday greeting. It was a private party; nobody else was invited. It was their own

hunk of bitter victory—for many were lost over Berlin, taking part of the *Luftwaffe* with them.

But Rosie, the pilot, had completed his tour of duty. The sky was filled with flares—the armament men had given them two extra boxes before take-off that morning. They threw the Fourth of July up at the cold gray sky; and the control tower, which is a grave and dignified institution at an airfield—something like the Supreme Court—came back with more flares.

The crew's request to the pilot that morning, when they learned it was to be Berlin, had been for a "beautiful buzz job" coming in. The pilot gave it to them with his low swoop over the tower. It is said—though J. E. Woodard, the husky crew chief denies it—that big tears rolled down his face when *Rosie's Riveters* showed at last over the tower.

Then the crew rode off in great style to the interrogation, each man on a jeep. All except T/Sgt. Michael V. Bocuzzi, the radio operator; he rode on the rear of a proud MP's motorcycle.

I SHOULDA ATE ALONE

By Pvt. SEYMOUR BLAU

So you finally got here. Well, it's about time. Keeping me waiting in a restaurant since 6 o'clock. What's the excuse this time? You had to get a gun from ordnance? Well, Lucy's husband is a sergeant, too, and it's funny he comes home every night at half past 5.

Hungry? I'm starved. I shoulda ate alone but I always wait for you like a sap. What am I doing in this terrible town anyway if you can't even eat *one* meal with me?

What happened? Well, the place got kinda crowded, and a captain and his wife wanted to know could they sit here, so I said why of course sit right down. I figgered as long as his wife was along I wouldn't get into a funny situation with a soldier like you're always growling about.

Steak; I want a decent meal for a change. No, I don't care one hoot about the bank account. I always have to pinch pennies. You're 10 times smarter than Janie's boy friend. Why can't you be a lieutenant?

Shhh! Darling, please don't make a scene. This is the only decent place in town. Awright, awright; that's enough; I'm sorry. I think you're wonderful anyway. Love me?

Mmmm. This soup is good. The captain? Oh. Well, I know you never try to push yourself ahead, you dildock, so when we got to talking I tried to *put in a good word for you. I figgered you never* can tell who a captain is. I was only thinking about you, dear, and nothing woulda happened if you hadn't left me alone like that.

I told him what a good sergeant you was, always taking care of the men and lettin' 'em go to town all the time and everything. And how they like you, and——

Why are you stopping eating, darling? What else did I say? Well, I told him how you never made the men walk too fast on a hike and always gave them plenty of time to rest their feet an' all. Then the captain said sometimes the men have to walk fast, and I said my husband says the time to walk fast is to chow, and they laughed. His wife was the prettiest thing and so nice, asking me did I have trouble finding a room and all. They live at the Town Hotel and pay $25 a week and have to furnish their own sheets.

Huh? Oh, I said you were really the smartest man in your company and how mad you got when things went wrong at camp and if they'd only listen to you everything would be okay.

By now they were putting their coats on, and I thought maybe he could get you a good desk job on the post where you could come home every night like Sally's husband.

So I asked the captain couldn't he use a good sergeant like you in his company, because, I said, my husband says that if there ever was an awful jerk it's his company commander.

What's your husband's name, the captain asked me. Sgt. Willie O. Smithley, I said. Is that so? said he. Sometimes I find out interesting things about my men in restaurants. I'm his company commander. So right away I said——

Darling, what are you standing there like that for? What did I do?

"Understand they're takin' it back to the States."
—Sgt. Ozzie St. George.

"Are you the athletic noncom?"—Sgt. Ozzie St. George.

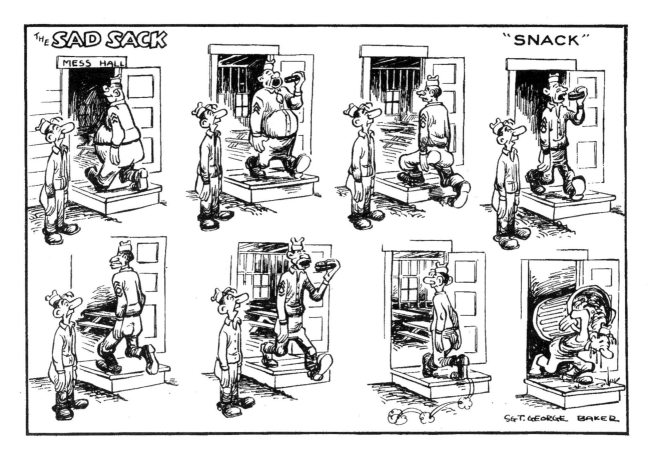

NOMENCLATURE OF WHISTLE, M1

By Pvt. RAYMOND ZAUBER

(Description of the simple air-cooled whistle, as done in GI handbook terms)

THE U. S. whistle, model M1, is a self-repeating, shoulder-strap model. It is lung-operated, air-cooled, reverberating-blast type. The whistle weighs an ounce and a half, and the chain another half ounce.

The whistle is divided into two parts—the whistle-cylinder blowing assembly, and the whistle-retaining chain assembly. At the blowing aperture there are two raised sections, one on each side, called the upper-teeth guard lug and the lower-teeth guard lug, respectively. The opening from the blowing end into the cylinder is known as the compressing-blow channel. The remainder of the whistle apparatus is known as the chamber-cylinder operating assembly. This consists of the opening-sound emission slot, the cylinder-butt lock onto which the whistle-retaining chain assembly is attached, and the cylinder-reverberating operating cork.

The whistle-retaining chain consists of the shoulder-strap button-hook catch which secures the whistle for carrying and operation. The shoulder-strap button-hook catch is locked by the upper-chain retaining ring. The chain is also fastened to the lower-chain retaining ring which is looped through the cylinder-butt lock of the whistle cylinder-blowing assembly.

The whistle is carried in the upper left pocket of the blouse or jacket. To use, unbutton or unsnap pocket with fingers of the right hand, remove whistle by raising directly up on retaining chain. When the whistle swings free of the pocket grasp the sides of the whistle-blowing assembly with the thumb and forefinger of the left hand and with the upper-teeth lug facing up and to the rear. Then place between the center of lips and clamp lips firmly so that no air can escape.

The sound is produced by taking a deep breath through the nostrils and exhaling it through the mouth into the air-compressing blow channel. After the blast return the whistle to the pocket by the reverse of the steps used for removal.

Disassembling of all parts, other than the shoulder-strap button-hook catch and the lower-chain retaining ring, is for ordnance only.

WHAT'S YOUR PROBLEM?

NAVY NUMERALS

Dear YANK:

A lot of Navy men I see have little numerals, like "1" and "2," pinned on their campaign ribbons. I think they signify the number of engagements the wearer has participated in, but my buddies aren't so sure I know what I'm talking about. Am I right?

Hawaii —JOE CURTIS S1c

You're wrong. Those numerals refer to the kinds of service the wearer has performed. The Navy has four kinds of service: escort, submarine, amphibian and patrol. If a sailor served on an escorting destroyer during a specific campaign and his destroyer was also engaged in amphibian landings, the numeral "2" on his ribbon would show that he had performed two kinds of service. Incidentally, you won't be seeing them any more; the Navy has decided to eliminate their use.

MEDICAL OPERATIONS

Dear YANK:

Just before I got into the Army I thought. I needed an operation, but my doctor told me not to have one because it would have after-effects worse than the ailment itself. Now the Army tells me I must have the operation, and when I protested, the Army doctor said I could be court-martialed for refusing. I don't think I should have any operation I don't need, and I want to know whether it is true that I can be court-martialed if I refuse?

Hawaii —PFC. FRANK G. PENDALL

Yes. AR 600-10 (2-e-9) states that refusal to submit to a dental or medical operation in time of war may result in court martial. If you really doubt the necessity of an operation, the matter will be referred to a three-man medical board, which decides whether the operation is necessary in order for you "to perform properly" your military duties. If they say operation, operation it is; and if you still say no, you may be tried by court martial.

REFUSING A DISCHARGE

Dear YANK:

What's my problem? Here it is. I was drafted in 1942 with a bad ankle. I was discharged with a CDD five months later. After being a civilian for only two months, I was drafted again. Now the Army wants to discharge me again; I have recently rejected two CDDs but I am up for a third, and this time the Army doctor tells me I won't be able to do anything about it and that I will have to ac-

cept the discharge. But that's pretty damned dumb. If I am released I will be drafted right away again, and I don't mind saying I'm pretty sick and tired of going through induction stations.

How can I stay in the Army, YANK, and save myself a lot of mess and bother?

Panama —CPL. ANTON LACHENBRUCH

If the Army doesn't want you, you're out. Your draft board might try to reinduct you into the Army, of course, but our guess is that it won't. Army physical standards today are probably at rock-bottom, and if Uncle Sam can't use you now, you almost certainly will be let alone from here on in. Incidentally, that must be one helluva bad ankle you've got.

FATHER AND SON

Dear YANK:

I've a problem that even Mr. Anthony couldn't solve. He wrote me and said to go and see my chaplain. Well, sir, it's this way. I met a girl in the States in 1939. She was living with a fellow, not legally married. In 1940 she gave birth to a baby boy, my son. But as I wasn't at her side, she gave the baby this fellow's name. Later he died. I was away at that time, too, and couldn't get back to her. Later she married, legally, another fellow. Then in 1942 this man committed an FBI crime. He's now serving his second year of a possible 10-year sentence. I've written to her, and she's willing to cooperate in any way to have my son's name changed to mine as I'm helping with his support. I'm still not married to my son's mother, and at this time she is living with yet another fellow and by September will give birth to his baby. Isn't there some way I can give my son my name without having to marry his mommy?

Britain —SGT. M. C. H.

In most states it is possible to change an official birth record to show the name of a child's real father. You did not mention the state in which your son was born, but if you tell your legal assistance officer he will be able to inform you just how to apply to the proper state authorities to get your son's record corrected.

RETURN TO OVERSEAS

Dear YANK:

I am 38 years old. They told me, when I was over in North Africa last summer, that I could get out of the Army if I applied for discharge before Aug. 1. I fulfilled all the requirements and eventually found myself hanging on the rail of a transport sailing for home. Well, YANK, when I saw Liberty's statue in New York Harbor—and I know this sounds corny —I got to regretting I was gonna be a civilian. And that's what I told my new CO; I told him I wanted to withdraw my application for discharge. He blew up like an ammunition dump. When the smoke cleared, I found out that he had orders fixed up for me to be shipped right back to the North African Theater—to my old command! At this very moment I'm looking at the transport that is probably going to take me back across the Atlantic. But what I'd like to know is, can this CO *legally* do this to me?

Port of Embarkation —S/SGT. JOE MORTON

He sure can. Ours is the sad duty to refer you to Sec. IV, WD Cir. No. 10, 6 Jan. 1944. Subparagraph 2 says that any man 38 years old serving overseas who has asked for a withdrawal of his approved application for discharge after he has already been returned to the States will be packed off in the first shipment heading back to his old command. One of the reasons for this circular, the Army says, is that some GIs were using the over-38 discharge rule, not as a way to get out of the Army, but simply as a pretext to get back to the States.

LOST TEETH

Dear YANK:

Does a GI have to sign a statement of charges if he loses the set of false teeth issued to him by the Army? Some guys say you do, and I'm worried. While we were crossing on the ship I was put on a detail as a sort of "bucket brigade" member who passes cardboard cases down to the galley below. One wise guy threw a box at my chest and the jolt bounced my false teeth into the Pacific. It wasn't my fault, and I'll be one damned sore dogface if I am expected to pay for them.

Australia —PVT. DOMINICK ATRELLIA

False teeth are not considered "property" in the usual sense of the word, and the Judge Advocate General has ruled that a GI who accidentally loses his dentures does not have to pay for them on a statement of charges.

ALLOTMENT MUDDLE

Dear YANK:

I have been overseas since June 1942. My pay was stopped in October 1942 because my mother was supposed to have been overpaid by the Office of Dependency Benefits. Since then I have had a few partial payments amounting to about $200.

Now the ODB has cut off my mother's allotment entirely. They have also cut off my 6-year-old son's allotment. My mother is 68 and in very poor health. I can't understand why I get no pay and why the allotments were cut off. I've tried writing to the ODB and seeing my first sergeant, but it doesn't do any good. What can I do to get some money?

Italy —NAME WITHHELD

You'd better get used to living on partial payments, brother; you owe the ODB a wad of dough. ODB's records show that your mother has been overpaid to the tune of $1,292. Here are the facts:

In May 1942 you made a Class E (voluntary) allotment of $25 a month to your mother. Later that month you discontinued that allotment and set up one for $45. Your orderly room failed to notify ODB about your discontinuing the $25 allotment, so ODB paid both amounts through September 1943, at which time the $45 allotment was stopped. The $25 check kept on going to your mother until January 1944. A third Class E allotment, based on an incorrect serial number, was also paid to your mother from October 1942 to September 1943. Total overpayment: $1,760.

You made out still another Class E allotment in June 1942 for $18 a month. The ODB never paid this one, however, so in theory at least they owe you $468. After this is deducted from the overpayments, you still owe ODB $1,292.

In January 1943 you applied for a Class F (family) allotment for your mother and son, retroactive to June 1942. This allotment was granted, costing you $27 a month back to June 1942, so that for over a year your mother received almost $200 a month in allotments. The ODB says that your wife, who you say died in 1941, is very much alive and has applied for a family allowance, claiming that your son lives with her. Your mother contends that the boy is with her. Both claims are being investigated now.

Don't worry, though. Money isn't everything.

TIRE RETREADERS

Dear YANK:

I am going nuts retreading tires. I am getting stale and despondent. Only YANK can help me. You see, I have always wanted to get into the Infantry, and when I heard about that new *WD Cir. 132* making it practically mandatory for COs to approve any GI's request for transfer into the Infantry I rocketed over to the Old Man here. Smiling blissfully, I told him to get me outa this unit pronto. Shocked, I heard him say he wouldn't let me transfer, and yet with my own eyes I had read in that circular where only the War Department could say "no" on such a deal. YANK, it's up to you now.

Aberdeen Proving Grounds, Md. —PVT. F. L. H.

Sorry, but we have to fail you. WD Memo. W615-44 (29 May 1944) lists tire rebuilders among the specialists who "are and have been for an extended period of time critically needed by the Army." The memorandum goes on to say that such critically needed specialists "may not volunteer for assignment and duty in the Infantry" under the provisions of Cir. 132.

CHANGING NAMES

Dear YANK:

The name. Just look at it! Can I change it, YANK? Can I?

Hawaii —PVT. WOLWOFF ZYLBERCWEICZ

Sure. But you'll have to see your Legal Assistance Officer, because authority to change your name is granted by the individual states and state laws vary. Generally the court requires a good reason—for example, "it is too long" or "people can't pronounce it" or "for business." To get your new name on the Army records, you must show your CO a certified copy of the court order. See WD Cir. 254 (1943), Sect. II.

GI "MINORS"

Dear YANK:

I enlisted in the Army while I was under age; I lied to the recruiting officer and served two years before I was discovered. The Army gave me an honorable discharge, however. Since then I have been drafted and am now nearing the end of my first "drafted" year. This, added to my earlier service, gives me three full years in the Army, but I have been told that I cannot wear a hash mark for that three-year hitch because I enlisted under false colors. I don't think that's fair. After all, I've done nothing I should be ashamed of.

Iran —PFC. JAMES N. HELLER

According to regulations, service stripes can be worn by those "who have served honorably," whether continuously or not, and the fact that you were discharged because you were under age does not bar you from wearing a service stripe. Your discharge is an honorable one, and that's what counts. Refer doubters to AR 615-360 (39) and AR 600-40 (46-e).

SHAVE AND HAIRCUT

Dear YANK:

I have a very serious problem that I would like your advice on. We are allowed to go to town in fatigues, mixed uniforms and practically anything we want. But can we grow a beard? Hell, no. I have started one four different times. They vary in length from five to 15 days. About that time a shave tail that isn't old enough to grow a beard pipes up: "Soldier, I will give you 30 minutes to get that beard shaved off." What we would like to know is, do soldiers overseas have the right to grow beards?

India —CPL. GLEN CARLSEN

That's a tough one. AR 40-205, Paragraph 7, says the soldier will keep ". . . the beard neatly trimmed." Looks to us as if you'll just have to hide in the jungle until your struggling whiskers get to where they can stand trimming. Even then it's our guess that most COs will insist that a "neatly trimmed" beard is simply a smooth shave.

Dear YANK:

. . . I prize my sideburns, but an officer just told me to get a GI haircut. Do I have to, YANK, when I see lots of guys with long hair?

Panama —PVT. SIDNEY MILLER

That's a little easier. The same AR says ". . . hair will be kept short." No room for question there. Those sideburns must go.

DRILLING SQUARE HOLES

Dear YANK:

Ever since I came into the Army I've been plagued by doubting Thomases when I told them what I did in civilian life, and I know I've lost out on some good deals because resentful officers thought I was pulling their legs when they interviewed me for various jobs. So YANK, if you will please put into print that fellows *can* make a living out of drilling square holes (and that this has no connection with left-handed monkey wrenches or sky-hooks), I will carry your clipping around as official protection against Army wise guys.

Australia —PVT. NICHOLAS KOMITO

Glad to help. As a matter of fact, there is a tool firm in Pennsylvania that drills square holes. A special drill has three lips, with the heel of each "land" rocking the drill so that it turns a corner as its lip finishes a side cut. The motion of the chuck enables the drill to move in alternate cycloid curves whose cords ——. But, say, this can go on for a long time. Suppose we just say you're right. Okay?

"I keep him here for slamming down the telephone."
Pfc. Aldo, Jefferson Barracks, Mo.

MEDAL FOR FROSTBITE

Dear YANK:

A guy up here, a private, was in on the landing at Attu and he wears a Purple Heart. Well, that's okay—or so I thought until I found out that he got that medal because he got frostbite during the invasion. YANK, I've heard lots of stories about GIs lining up to get medals from a barrel the way we sweat out servings of stew, but I always rejected those stories as some of Goebbels' wildest fancies. I'm still skeptical. Just what authority says that an American decoration like the Purple Heart, which is often given posthumously to men killed in action, can be handed out for—heaven help us—frostbite?

Alaska   —PFC. J. L. HENDRICKS

AR 600-45, Changes 4 (3 May 1944) says that the Purple Heart may be awarded to personnel wounded in action, "provided such wound necessitates treatment by a medical officer," and defines a wound "as an injury to any part of the body from an outside force, element or agent." The word "element," according to the AR, refers to weather and permits award of the Purple Heart to personnel severely frostbitten while actually engaged in combat. Incidentally, severe frostbite is a pretty serious business and sometimes results in amputation.

CRAPS AND CONSCIENCE

Dear YANK:

I come from the backwoods of North Dakota. I had never seen a crap game until I entered the service. When I saw my first game back in the States I joined in, just for the fun of it. It came my turn to shoot the dice. I shot $5 and made an "11." One of the boys told me this was an easy point to make, so I rolled again. The boys all offered to bet me I wouldn't make "11" again. The sergeant bet me $10 I couldn't make "11" on the next roll. I accepted all bets on this "11" and made it—breaking all my buddies, including the sergeant. After reading the gambling articles in YANK, I now realize that "11" was no point to roll for and that I should have won my $5 on the first roll. I also realize that making an "11" on one roll is a 17-1 bet. So here is my problem. Shall I return the money to my buddies, who I now see were trying to take advantage of me, or shall I keep it? Oh yes, I forgot to mention that I can throw an "11" any time I desire. I learned to do it while playing parchesi back home in Ellenville, N. Dak.

Iran   —PVT. J. H. R.

Why write to What's Your Problem? *Any guy who shoots an "11" anytime he wants to can't possibly have any problems.*

BENEFITS FOR GIRL FRIENDS?

Dear YANK:

I have a problem and any help you can give me in solving it will be plenty appreciated. But please don't use my name. Shortly after I was inducted, my wife and I agreed to separate, but we didn't get a divorce. Sometime later I started living with another woman. Of course, I'm not married to this woman, but not long ago she applied for and received, with my knowledge and approval, a family allowance as my wife. Now I've been worrying about this lately because I've got a good idea that my legal wife is going to apply for an allowance also. If that happens, what can they do to the girl friend?

India   —CPL. O. T. R.

Brother, you'd better sit down in a hurry and write that girl friend a long letter. And the first thing you should tell her is to beg or borrow enough money pronto to pay back every cent that she has received in allowances from the Office of Dependency Benefits. Then she should send that dough together with a full and frank confession of her unenviable position to the Allowances Branch, ODB, 213 Washington Street, Newark, N. J.

What can they do to the girl friend? Mac, they can stuff the book right down her throat. What's more, if you helped her in the fraud, they can gag you with a couple of pages yourself. See Public Law 625—77th Congress; Bull. 29, W. D., 1942. Sec. 116: "Whoever shall obtain or receive any money, check, or family allowance . . . without being entitled thereto and with intent to defraud, shall be punished by a fine of not more than $2,000, or by imprisonment for not more than one year, or both." Sec. 117: "Whoever in any claim for family allowance or in any document required . . . makes any statement of a material fact knowing it to be false, shall be guilty of perjury and shall be punished by a fine of not more than $5,000, or by imprisonment for not more than two years, or both."

Come to think about it, mark that letter "Registered—Air Mail—Special Delivery."

FAITHLESS WIFE

Dear YANK:

I am enclosing the exact wording of a letter sent me by wife and will be ever grateful for any possible solution, for I have tried everything I know, even prayer. Still TS. Question: Can wife get allotment without consent of me when I have this letter of bad faith? Here are her words:

Dear Ahmed—The time has come to clear things between us. You will have realized, before now, that our marriage was a mistake. I beg of you to put an end to this mistake and get a divorce. I left your house this morning, because I didn't want to saddle you with the role of a betrayed husband. As a matter of fact, I have never been yours, but now I belong to someone else, and this finishes things between us.

I have grown distrustful of what is generally known as "love," for the feelings that have alienated me from you are drawn elsewhere, and I've got to obey the secret promptings of my nerves. I want to thank you and wish you well. I am going away. It makes me unhappy to hurt you, but you are so strong. I am still your friend, and perhaps the time will come when you can be my friend, too. I am taking everything except your clothes and the typewriter, and am having my friend type this for me, for you know I write poorly.—ELAINE.

Iran   —PFC. AHMED S.

Yours is simply a classic version of a common problem. All the proof in the world that a soldier's wife is faithless does not change the fact that a family allowance is given to her regularly as long as she remains legally married to the soldier. If you are interested in initiating divorce proceedings you should consult your Legal Assistance Officer, who can give you information about the divorce laws in your state.

MAXIMUM FINES

Dear YANK:

I have been court-martialed three times in special court, twice for AWOL and once for assault. The assault was merely a tussle with another soldier. In June 1943 I was fined $30 a month for six months. On July 22 I was tried for the second offense and was fined $33 for six months. Two days later I was fined $33 for another six months. The court fined me two-thirds of my pay, but they have been taking all of it. Since June 1943, I have only received $10. This was when I was at the POE. What I would like to know is this: Is it lawful for the Army to take all of your money, allowing you nothing for cigarettes, etc.?

Guadalcanal   —PVT. RICHARD MACK

The Manual for Courts Martial [par. 104 (b), page 96] protects a man from having more than two-thirds of his pay taken away at any one time. Moreover a Judge Advocate ruling on that question makes it very clear that a GI may have no more than two-thirds of his pay taken away through action of a court martial unless the sentence of the court martial also orders a dishonorable discharge, and you have not been dishonorably discharged. Refer your Finance Officer to AR 35-2460 [par. 5(b)], and he will see to it that you get the money that is legally yours.

MEXICAN MUDDLE

Dear YANK:

I'll start from the very beginning. I'm 27 years old and I entered the Army in '41. While I was at Fort Sam Houston, Tex., I became infatuated with a girl and went to Mexico and was told by a priest (or monk) there that we were married by him. I lived with her only one night. There were no papers of the marriage, and I did not sign any such papers in Mexico. I paid her no allotment till June 1942 when, unknown to me, she applied for allotment. OK. In June 1943 I again went to Mexico and got a divorce (so I was told), but not one paper was signed by me or anyone else, for it was granted by this monk (or priest, or whatever he was) in Mexico.

I went to my first sergeant in my last camp to find out about getting the allotment to stop but failed. You see, this 70- or 80-year-old monk (or whatever he was) told me I'd have to pay her alimony. But me going to all the trouble I did, and with no one who could (or would) tell me anything, I went ahead and got married to another girl. Now I can't get an allotment for my second wife because of this other mess. I was told the first girl was married again and living in Mexico—where I do not know. I don't even know what happened to her, but they have been taking pay out of my $50 every month. Now, if my divorce was not legal how can the marriage be legal? Also where and how and when did she get papers asking for the allotment? Please can you help me as I'm in enough trouble as it is and do not want to lose the one girl I will really ever love. Several people here are calling me a bigamist, and I don't think I am.

Panama   —PVT. J. C. H.

Wow! Well, here goes. In the first place, as far as the allowance is concerned, that first girl was pretty smart, because she obviously submitted a marriage certificate of some kind to prove that she was your wife; otherwise the Office of Dependency Benefits would not have approved her application for a family allowance. In the second place, many foreign divorces are looked upon with deep suspicion by the ODB, and where there is not even documentary proof of the divorce (as in your case) the ODB would probably have to continue payments to the girl in Mexico. The ODB suggests you send full details of your case to its office at 213 Washington Street, Newark, N. J. Don't forget to include your ASN. As for the legal, social and moral aspects of your problem, see your Legal Assistance Officer. See your CO. See your personal affairs officer. See your chaplain. Quick.

Your letters to me

in response to
newspaper articles

SERVICE MEN'S STATIONERY KIT & SECRETARY

Free Mail Information

AMONG ITEMS ACCEPTABLE FREE OF POSTAGE ARE THE FOLLOWING:

Personal letters to relatives, friends, etc., including V-Mail.

Letters, including remittances, to associations, firms, or corporations.

Letters sent as special delivery, provided the fee for such service is pre-paid.

Small photographic negatives and unmounted prints when accompanying letters.

Souvenir and pictorial cards, unless bearing matters of a promotional character.

Greeting cards such as Mother's Day, birthday, seasonabl etc., enclosed in envelopes.

Election ballots.

Letters mailed while the sender is on furlough.

Letters sent by the midshipmen of the United States Naval Academy, the cadets of the United States Military Academy, and the cadets of the United States Coast Guard Academy.

Letters sent by retired or Reserve naval and Army officers who have been recalled to active duty, including those bearing the designation "U.S.N Ret." or "U.S.N.R." in connection with the name and rank or rating of such officer on active duty.

Letters sent by members of the armed forces while in hospitals.

Letters from members of the armed forces who may be assigned to some special active duty.

Letters from nurses and chaplains who are members of the armed forces

THE FREE MAIL PRIVILEGE DOES NOT APPLY TO THE FOLLOWING

Air mail.

Registered, insured, or c. o. d. mail.

Parcels or packages, whether sealed or unsealed.

Newspapers, magazines, and books.

Circular letters.

Newspaper clippings, and printed or mimeographed matter, unless enclosed with letters and forming only an incidental feature.

Cards exceeding the post-card size consisting mainly of cartoons or other printed matter.

Pictorial folders.

Envelopes and cards containing extraneous printed matter, stickers, etc., on the face.

Matter sent for philatelic purposes.

Merchandise.

Wedding invitations or announcements

Phonograph records.

Photographic films sent for development.

Large mounted photographs.

Letters of officers' clubs and other organizations.

Cards and envelopes bearing advertisements or other inscriptions giving the names of the donors.

Letters from persons in veterans hospitals who are not members of the armed forces.

Letters, bills, and circulars pertaining to the private business or profession carried on by a member of the armed forces.

Envelopes or cards endorsed by a member of the armed forces for use by others, such as members of his family, etc.

My Unlucky Shot

How was it possible? How could any man shoot himself in that most vital part of his anatomy, let alone one who was an expert marksman, a former small arms instructor and a company commander of an assault company of Marines in an attack situation?

My company had just overrun its objective, Hill 53 on Okinawa on June 11th, 1945. We had the enemy bottled up in caves, one of which occupied my attention. Joe Rhodes, our demolition sergeant threw in a satchel charge of dynamite and I followed it with a grenade and a foolish plunge into the cave. It should have been over but one survivor remained. In the dim light I saw the Japanese lieutenant crawling up onto his feet. Armed with only my 45 pistol I fired point blank. A sudden blow in that tenderest of regions brought me to my knees. I stumbled out of that cave thinking I had been shot in turn by that enemy lieutenant. One of my men examining the Jap's helmet noted my bullet had caved it in and the bullet had ricocheted back to strike me. In several minutes I was fully recovered and the possessor of a fine Samurai sword and Sergeant Rhodes had secured the small Japanese flag from within that helmet.

Many years have now gone by and many have been the times I have startled friends with the story of how I shot myself. "Daddy, what did you do in the war?" My dubious exploit that day which proved entertaining, always bothered me, however. I had the feeling some of my listeners doubted my truth. I had no witnesses or corroboration. This was simply my story; take it or leave it !

One evening in July of 1985 a long distance inquiry from Iowa. was to make me an honest man. A voice from the past, Joe Rhodes of forty years ago had located me. I don't know which thrilled me more, reestablishing contact with my trusted old Marine sergeant or now having confirmation and back-up for my wild story. At later reunions of the 6th Marine Division Joe would delight his listeners of the exploits of his stupid souvenier-hunting captain. But he did exact a promise from me, to will him that Samurai sword which he coveted. I in turn made an agreement with Joe: He to will me that Jap flag.

Today, the hilarity is gone from my story. The Samurai sword hangs from my wall, and below it is a small Jap flag. Joe died five years ago.

Frank H. Hagler, M.D.
Fullerton, CA

May 8, 1995

Mr. Leonard Zerlin
3232 Lanier Place
Thousand Oaks, CA 91360

Dear Mr. Zerlin:

A writer for The Dallas Morning News, March 21, 1995, had
a nice column about you and your effort to compile a list
of seasoning words used during WW2. Although I clipped the
article with every intention of responding promptly, time
passes.... Anyway, what better day than today, V-E day, to
finally jot down a few items?

On shortwave the German Radio sometimes referred to Franklin
Delano Roosevelt as "FRANKLIN STALINO ROSENFELD". Of course
we had midwest Republicans who did about the same thing.

As soon as Germany surrendered radio stations opened up in
Europe broadcasting on the AM band, and on shortwave, to
the GI's. The Armed Forces Network, "The Twin Voices of
Southern Germany: Munich-Stuttgart" operated on 1249KCS and
8.565MCS daytime and 6.080 nighttime. One popular program
was "Midnight in Germany" originating in several locations
with Disk Jockeys playing records on "Luncheon in Munchen",
"Madhouse in Munich", "Bouncing in Bavaria", etc. Each
program tried to outdo the other. One boasted, "Three more
records heard each hour than on any other one hour program".
Easy to do--just start selection number 2 before number 1 is
finished.

Every evening there were requests for ASSS. This was under-
stood to be "Avocado Sea Soup Symphony". As music it sounded
to me like two or three guys pounding on a box or desk for
five minutes; periodically someone would sing out "chug,
chug, chug, aaah rooooteee, aaah toooteee", and "Kelly
Motors, Duz Duz everything, eighteen full weeks to pay".
Invariably, the jockey would be swamped with requests for
ASSS Opus 2. And another five minutes would go by with box
pounding, "chug, chug, chug, aaah roooteee, aaah toooteee,
etc." To my untrained ears Opus 2 sounded exactly like
Opus 1.

Are these little items of interest to you? If so, be my
guest and use them if you like. (The above comes from many
pages of notes I kept during the war.)

                              Best regards,

                              W. E. Keller
                              2026 Misty Glen Trail #320
                              Arlington, TX 76011

Robert S. Babin
26822 Hawkhurst Dr.
Rancho P.V. CA 90275

30 April 1995

Dear Mr. Zerlin,

In reply to your letter in today's Times:

Thinking back to my 1944-5 hitch in the U.S. Navy, I recall a vivid expression heard repeatedly in and around the shower room, while we were preparing to go out on liberty. Typically this would be late on a Friday afternoon, when we young men were all anticipating leaving the base and were salivating over the likelihood of getting some booze and babes, in that sequence. The alliterative expression was

"Now I gotta shit, shower, shampoo, shave, and shine."

I like your phrase "For those of us who still have our faculties...before we start looking up at the roses." I am age 70.

May your book sell like hotcakes.

Sincerely,

[signature]

The Borrelli Story

We have all had amazing incidents and coincidences which have occurred to us in our lifetimes. While most have faded in time, to be forgotten, some have remained in our memories, never to be forgotten, and in some cases perhaps, not believed by others when we have had occasion to recount such events.

During the assault and capture of Okinawa in the spring of 1945 in WW 2 I was a company commander in the 6th Marine Division. Following the war I resigned my commission and continued on with my education, completing medical school at the University of Illinois in 1950 and subsequently serving in the navy as a medical officer until 1952 when I commenced a fellowship in obstetrics and gynecology at the Mayo Clinic in Rochester, Minnesota.

It was in late January or early February of 1952 when during one of my "routine gynecology clinic " days on S-7 of the clinic diagnostic building I was assigned a new patient just arrived at the clinic from Southern California, a Mrs. Lucy Borrelli. Prior to my examination I inquired of Mrs. Borrelli as to her past medical history and related family as it may pertain to her current illness. Mrs. Borrelli informed me her family was all living and well with the exception of her oldest son who had been killed in the war. I expressed sympathy and asked conversationally how he had died and was informed he had been a marine corporal and had died near the end of the war on some island, Okinawa? This startled me and I asked if her former residence had been in Jersey City, New Jersey. "Yes", she said. "We used to live there but we moved to El Monte, California several months ago". I asked Mrs. Borrelli if her son wasn't Corporal Sam Borrelli of L Company, 3d Battalion, 22nd Marine regiment of the 6th Division. "Yes, she said. My boy Sam" and I said, "Mrs. Borrelli, your son was killed in action on May 15th on Okinawa". She asked how I knew that. I asked her if she had received a Christmas card from her son's former company commander every year since then to which she replied, "Yes, we get a card every year from some former marine captain". "Well, Mrs. Borrelli, that person is me: I'm a doctor now here at Mayo's" Needless to say, I was as startled as Mrs. Borrelli. Here among over 200,000 patients and me only one of probably 800 physicians I had encountered the mother of one of my boys I had lost in combat. I am not certain of that 200,000 patient census for that year but nevertheless, the chance of my being assigned that patient and then nearly missing the coincidence except for my having asked about the death of her son is indeed a rare possibility.

I was able, that evening, to visit her in the motel she was staying with. I had my old combat maps to show her the exact location where Sam had been killed, the photos of the division cemetery where he was buried at that time, and photos of his platoon showing him with his buddies, pictures she had never seen. I know it saddened her but it also answered questions she had always had and helped to close the book on her fine son. And I could assure her, I could not have asked for a finer Marine.

Frank H. Hagler, M.D.
Fullerton, CA

FROM the DESK of

al hix

15 May 95

Dear Mr Zerlin-

Saw your letter in the L A <u>Times</u> Book Review section. Your Vets'
fund-raising booklet is a great idea. Let me know where and when
I can buy one.

Was in the service from Mar '41 to Sept '45. Signal Corps attached
to the Air Corps/Force in such places as New Orleans Army Air Base,
Atcham & Tangmere Airdromes in the UK, bases all across No Africa,
then to Naples & Torre Maggiore in Italy.

Understandably, most of my singing or joking memories are from England,
where, for a time, we were attached to RAF groups before our own units
arrived. Do remember this oldie from when we were on maneuvers in
New Orleans:

Corporal: "Sorry, ma'am, you can't cross this bridge; it's just been
knocked out by the Blue Army."

The lady appeals to a passing sergeant, who says: "Sorry, ma'am, can't
help you. I've been dead for two days."

(Guess I should have explained that the above bridge was untouched. It
 had just been tactically destroyed on paper by one side in the maneuvers.
 Didn't know how familiar you were with maneuvers.)

Have always wondered whether there really was a song back then entitled
"I've Got Tears in my Ears from Lying on my Back in my Sack Crying
Over You."

Altho' it's derogatory, always had to grin when some Italians pronounced
"Americani" as "Merda Cane" (dog shit).

Good luck with the booklet! When I hear from my RAF chum or think of
anything else, shall write.

Cheers,

Al Hix

Al Hix,
2074 Glencoe Way
Hollywood, CA 90068
(213) 851-0316

This one was a favorite with the RAF:

CATS ON THE ROOFTOP

Cats on the rooftop, cats on the tiles,
Cats with the syphilis,cats with the piles,
Cats with their assholes wreathed in smiles,
As they revel in the joys of copulation.

Now the elephant is a funny, funny bloke,
He very, very seldom gets his poke,
But when he does, he lets it soak,
As he revels in the joys of copulation.

l'envoi

Oh, the hippotamus, so it seems,
Very, very seldom has wet dreams,
But when he does, it comes in streams,
As he revels in the joys of copulation.

l'envoi

There are many other verses, and I've asked an RAF chum IF he
remembers them.

# # # # # #

We in the Signal Corps even had our own cheer:

    Three dits, four dits, two dits, dah!
    Signal Corps, Signal Corps, Rah! Rah! Rah!

(In Morse, ... _ spells "shit.")

My father, who was in WWI Artillery, taught me their song:

    Over hill, over dale, as we hit the dusty trail
    And the caissons go rolling along.
    In and out, all around, as we tramp the dusty ground,
    And the caissons go rolling along.
    So it's hi, hi, hee, the Field Artillery,
    Shout our your numbers loud and strong -- hut, two three, four!
    And where e'er we go, the huns will always know
    That the caissons go rolling along.

# # # # # #

And whenever we sang the Army Air Corps (as it was when I went into
the service) song, the last line was:

"...nothing can stop the Army Air Corps (except the weather), nothing
 can stop the Army Air Corps!"

And our gag about those Brit barrage balloons, which were there to dis-
courage strafing or low-level bombing, was "If they ever cut those
cables, this whole friggin' island will sink."

# # # # # #

I'VE GOT SIXPENCE

I've got sixpence, jolly, jolly sixpence
I've got sixpence to last me all my life.
I've got tuppence to spend, tuppence to lend
And tuppence to send home to me wife.

No cares have I to grieve me
No pretty little girl to deceive me,
I'm happy as a king, believe me,
As I go rolling home.

Rolling home, dead drunk,
Rolling home, dead drunk,
By the light of the silvery moon.

Happy is the day when the airman gets his pay,
And we go rolling, rolling home.

I've got fourpence, jolly, jolly fourpence
I've got fourpence to last me all my life.
I've got tuppence to spend, tuppence to lend
and fuck-all to sent home to me wife.

l'envoi

(Then I've got tuppence with fuck-all to lend or send home, and
 if the pints are going down smoothly, we can get down to "no-pence."

# # # # #

Here's one that's sung to the tune of "The Colonel Bogie March" in a
Cockney accent:

"'Itler, 'e only 'as one ba'
 Goering 'as two but very sma'
 'Immler 'as something similar,
 But Dr Goebbels 'as no ba's at all."

♯ ♯ ♯ ♯ ♯ ♯

Then there was:

Dirty Gerty from Bizerte
Put a mousetrap up her skirty
Made her boyfriends' fingers hurty
Dirty Gerty from Bizerte.

There may have been more, but I don't remember it.

# # # # # #

What I remember about "Roll Me Over in the Clover" in the UK
was that it was "Roll Me Over, Yankee Soldier."

And I loved that succinct expression: "Blow it out your barracks
bag!"

Dr. Allan S. Nanes

International Affairs
Terrorism
U.S. Foreign Policy

60 W. Easy Street #3
Simi Valley, CA 93065

Phone (805) 579-7920
Fax (805) 522-6343

May 6, 1995

Leonard Zerlin,
3232 Lanier Place,
Thousand Oaks, CA 91360

Dear Leonard,

I'm the guy who called you Thursday night mentioning that I had seen your letter in the Book Review section of last Sunday's L.A. Times. I'm living at 67 Triangle Street in Thousand Oaks, and this stationery is from an office I sublet in Simi Valley. I really have no income from this would-be consulting business, but I do have some part time earnings from my job in Koreatown writing newspaper editorials and other materials, which I think I mentioned in our phone conversation.

During WWII I was stationed in India with the 20th Air Force, 468th Bomb Group, 793rd Bomb Squadron. I was what we called a "chairborne airman," namely an operations clerk. I kept up all the operational files and typed the correspondence, including the letters of consolation when a plane didn't come back. The 20th Air Force was the first unit to fly the B-29's, and it was composed of pilots who had lots of hours in B-24's, plus crews that trained in Arizona, Kansas, and California.

We arrived in India in April of 1944, stayed there about a year, and then were moved to the Marianas, winding up on Tinian. We bombed Japan from both places, and Japanese controlled territory in Manchuria and Southeast Asia. There were forward bases in Chengtu, China, and many of our personnel were transferred there within a few months of arriving in India. I was slated to go, but my orders were changed. I can't say I'm sorry, because B-29's were slamming into the Hump (Himalayas) all the time.

Also stationed on Tinian was the 509th Composite Bomb Group, which turned out ※※※ to be the outfit that dropped the atomic bomb. We didn't know what they were, but they were reputed to be some kind of a special outfit. A couple of B-29's lumbering to get airborne just smashed into the Pacific, and after the a-bomb was dropped I used to sweat thinking about what could have happened to us had any A-bomber met this fate. The whole island would have been incinerated and drowned at the same time. Anyway, we were transferred once again to Saipan,※※※※※※※※※※ from which we were ※※※ sent home according to the point system. I was discharged in November of 1945.

All I have to offer your collection is a parody, written by a member of the 793rd Bomb Squadron, to the tune of Remember Pearl Harbor. Its on the next page.

Best regards,

Allan S. Nanes
379-1578

```
                    Let's Remember Salua

Let's remember Salua,
Where we died for a three day pass,

Let's remember Salua,
You can shove it up your ass.

Where the captains made major,
And the majors colonel, too.

But the pfc's and privates,
And the corporals, fuck you.


                                    Alan S. Nanes
```

Sgt. Al Dietrick
B. Co. 141 Inf.

PFC Al Dietrick

The picture on the left was taken about **22 Sept. 1943** at Altavilla, Italy. The picture on the right was taken 51 years later on **17 May 1994** at the same identical spot. (You remember wht PFC stands for?) I can't print it.

ANZIO BEACHHEAD

JANUARY 22, 1944 – MAY 25, 1944

HELL'S HALF ACRE

STANLEY R. SMITH
163 LYMAN STREET
WESTBOROUGH, MA 01581-2619
PHONE (508) 366 - 9790
THIRD INFANTRY DIVISION
"ROCK OF THE MARNE -- NOUS RESTERONS LA" (WE'RE STAYING HERE)
ANZIO MOTTO --- "STAND AND FIGHT"

DEAR MR. ZERLIN,   5 MAY 1995

THOUGHT OF A FEW MORE PHRASES THAT YOU ASKED FOR IN THE "PURPLE HEART"

MAGAZINE MARCH - APRIL 1995.

HEADED WHEN WE ARRIVED AT THE INDUCTION CENTER: "YOU'LL BE SORRY!!"

"WATCH THE SQUARE NEEDLE WITH THE HOOK ON THE END OF IT!!"

STORY: WHEN I JOINED THE THIRD INFANTRY DIVISION ON JANUARY 19, 1944, THREE BE

FORE THE LANDING AT THE ANZIO BEACHHEAD IN ITALY. THE PLATOON SGT. WANTED

TO SEE HIS NEWEST ROOKIE (JUST A SNOT NOSED KID OF 19 FROM THE STATE OF

MAINE). HE STARTED WITH HAD I HAD BASIC AND HOW LONG. TOLD THAT I HAD 13

WEEKS IN THE FOURTH PLATOON IN A LIGHT MACHINE GUN SQUAD. HE SAID DID I

QUALIFY WITH THE M-1 AND I SAID THAT I HAD. HE SAID,"YOU SEE THAT GOD DAMNED

M-1 LEANING AGAINST THE TENT POLE?" SAID THAT I DID. THEN HE SAID, "WELL YOU

GO AND GRAB IT, BECAUSE YOU ARE A GOD DAMNED RIFLEMAN NOW!" (THIS WAS THE

3rd PLATOON OF COMPANY I 30th INF. REGT.). THE NEXT THING HE SAID I HAVE NEVER

FORGOTTEN EVEN AFTER OVER FIFTY YEARS -- "KID, THERE ARE TWO MEN ON THE

FRONT LINE - THE QUICK AND THE DEAD!" OH, HOW RIGHT HE TURNED OUT TO BE!!!!

MY PARTING STATEMENT WAS THAT I HAD NEVER HAD ANY LANDING TRAINING. HE

SHOT BACK WITH, "DON'T WORRY ABOUT IT, KID, WE ARE GOING TO GIVE YOU SOME 'ON

THE JOB TRAINING'!! (SURE THE HELL GOT THAT TRAINING THE EARLY MORNING HOURS OF JANUARY 23, 1944!).

THIS SGT. WAS AN OLDER MAN THAT HAD BEEN WITH THE DIVISION BACK IN THE STATES HAD BEEN THROUGH THE NORTH AFRICAN , SICILIAN, AND ITALIAN CAMPAIGN. IF THERE WAS A TYPICAL ARMY SGT. HE WAS <u>IT</u>-- ROUGH, TOUGH, BUT FAIR! THE LAST TIME I SAW HIM WAS MAY 23, 1944 THE FIRST DAY OF THE ATTACK TO BREAKOUT OF THE ANZIO BEACHHEAD. EARLY THAT AFTERNOON I GOT HIT THE SECOND TIME--THE FIRST TIME WAS FEBRUARY 6, 1944. HAVE HEARD THE STORY THAT IN MARCH OR APRIL THE SGT. STEPPED ON A MINE AND LOST BOTH LEGS AND HE SURVIVED. SURE HOPE SO, BECAUSE HE HAD A VERY PROFOUND INFLUENCE ON MY LIFE.

THIS IS JUST ONE OF THE MANY STORIES I HAVE - NOT TOO MUCH TIME SPENT IN COMBAT, BUT OVER TWO AND A HALF YEARS IN U.S. ARMY HOSPITALS-----DISCHARGED FROM THE HOSPITAL AND ARMY SEPTEMBER 13, 1946!

THANK YOU.

SINCERELY YOURS,

STANLEY R. SMITH

NATIONAL MEMBERSHIP CHAIRMAN

"SOCIETY OF THE THIRD INFANTRY

DIVISION"

14 Beverly Lane
Shelton, Connecticut 06484
April 24, 1995

Mr. Leonard Zerlin
3232 Lanier Place
Thousand Oaks, California 91360

Dear Mr. Zerlin:

I am writing to you about your letter which appeared in the
Military Order of the Purple Heart Magazine (March-April 1995,
Vol. LVII, No. 2).

My father, George E. Bartram (Pfc., 329th, 3rd Bn., HQ Co.),
served in the United States Army with the 83rd Infantry Division
(ETO), during World War II. He has the Purple Heart (and belongs
to the M.O.P.H.), Bronze Star, Combat Infantry Badge (CIB),
five (5) Battle Stars and several other medals.

I have looked through the magazines (Life, Air News, and several
others) which my father has here. I also looked through the
"Thunderbolt" magazine, the official publication of the 83rd
Infantry Division.

Attached are several things which you might be able to use in
your book. Your idea of collecting songs, phrases and certain
words which were used during World War II, is a very good one.
Hope I have sent you some things that you can use and are not
repeats of someone else.

Thank you for serving this country. I sincerely appreciate
the wonderful gift all the Veterans gave me and millions of other
Americans - OUR FREEDOM!!! I will continue to look for anything
else which I think you might be able to use in your book.

Please contact me when you finish the book, as I would like to
purchase a copy.

                    Sincerely,

                    Roberta A. Pilloise
                    (George Bartram's daughter)

P.S. Yes, my father is still alive and in very good health!

Here are some phrases used in and during World War II -

Back the Attack

"Got any gum, chum?"

Any bonds today?

We work for victory, we plan for peace

Excellence in war production

Victory Garden

"V" Mail

The following are from Sal Scicolone's records from Camp Atterbury, Indiana - 1942.

(These were both printed in "Thunderbolt" magazine, 83rd Infantry Division Association, Inc., World War II - Vol. 47, No. 3, Spring 1992 Edition)

CAMP ATTERBURY INDIANA - 1942

We are the thundering herd from the 83rd
and fighting men are we.
We'll slap the maps of the dirty Japs
and march through Germany!

And when you see a man on leave
with the triangle on his sleeve,
You can tell he's a bird from the 83rd
and a fighting Son of a B!

When we go into combat
we'll meet them with knife and gun,
They'll no sooner see us coming
than we'll have them on the run!

And if you need a fighting man,
just raise your voice and yell--
You'll get a bird from the 83rd
who'll knock them straight to hell!

MEN OF THE 83RD

We are the men of the 83rd
We are the men who will keep our word
We were born in Ohio
And raised all over the land
And now we've got together
We make a damn good band - Oh
We like to march with a song and a gun
We like to fight, we do it for fun
We'll get the Jap and the Germans yet
And stick 'em all with a bayonet - Oh
We are the men of the 83rd.

STANLEY R. SMITH
163 LYMAN STREET
WESTBOROUGH, MA 01581- 2619
PHONE (508) 366 - 9790
"ROCK OF THE MARNE - NOUS RESTERONS LA"
(WE'RE STAYING HERE)

DEAR SIR,   *4 MAY 1995*

SAW YOUR REQUEST FOR ITEMS, SONGS, PHRASES-- FROM WORLD WAR 2.

ENCLOSED PLEASE FIND SONG AND LYRICS OF THE SONG THAT WAS TAKEN OVER AND

STILL IS A VERY IMPORTANT PART OF THE "THIRD INFANTRY DIVISION"

JUST FOR THE HELL OF IT WE WOULD CHANGE THE LAST LINE, WHILE AT THE ANZIO

BEACHHEAD IN 1944: "SO GIVE MY AMMUNITION TO THE 45th DIVISION AND SEND ME

BACK TO THE GOOD OLD U.S.A.!".

ALWAYS REMEMBER THE NIGHT OF MAY 21, 1944 WHEN WE LEFT "THE PINES" TO

RETURN TO THE FRONT LINE FOR THE LARGE ATTACK TO BREAKOUT OF ANZIO. THE

DIVISION BAND WERE LINED UP BY THE SIDE OF THE ROAD AND PLAYED "DOG-FACE

SOLDIER" AS THE WHOLE DAMNED DIVISION MARCHED BY ON THERE WAY UP FRONT!!

THEY MUST HAVE PLAYED MOST OF THE NIGHT!!!

AT OUR REUNIONS EACH YEAR, AFTER THE BANQUET AND WHEN THE DANCING STARTS

THE FIRST SONG PLAYED IS "DOG-FACE SOLDIER"!

THANK YOU AND THE VERY BEST OF LUCK IN YOUR ENDOVER.

                                        "ROCK OF THE MARNE"
                                        STANLEY R. SMITH

(COMPANY I 30th INF. REGT. WW-2)

30 April 1995

Mr. Leonard Zerlin
3232 Lanier Place
Thousand Oaks CA 91360

Dear Mr. Zerlin:

This is in response to your request in the LA Times Book Review today for "expressions, sayings and songs that were part of our service experiences."

I went through the Aviation Cadet program at Yale University in 1943. I of course do not know the particular arrangements, but in effect Yale rented to the Army, as its own student body dwindled as a result of the war. In the case of Aviation Cadets, physical training was the only instruction given by Yale staff members. In the case of the Army Specialized Training Program, I believe that most (perhaps all) instruction was given by Yale staff members. The ASTP personnel were being trained, I believe, as interpreters, translators, intelligence specialists, etc.

There was a marked difference in the military appearance as between Aviation Cadets (a West Point attitude) and ASTP privates (almost a pre-hippie condition, as we observed it). Thus the following song verse expresses derision based upon both a feeling of military superiority and a premise that the ASTP personnel would never be in combat danger. As soon as the verse became known to officialdom, an order was issued to forbid its being sung any more, while marching in formation.

Father is over the ocean
And sister is over the sea
But mother, don't worry 'bout junior
For he's is the ASTP

Bring back, bring back, oh bring my Johnnie to me, to me
Bring back, bring back, bring back my Johnnie to me

He uses his desk for a fox hole
The only one he'll ever see
So mother, don't worry 'bout junior
For he's in the ASTP

Bring back, bring back, oh bring my Johnnie to me, to me
Bring back, bring back, bring back my Johnnie to me

The other verse expressed the esprit de corps of the Aviation Cadets, and was frequently sung during marching. Most such singing, however, involved standard tunes, from "Over There" to "I've Got Sixpence." This verse had its own tune, not an adaptation of any existing tune to new words. I cannot read music, so I cannot express the tune for you, although I could still sing it with my off-key voice.

You have heard of the pilot so daring
As he gracefully flies through the air
But without all the men in the hangars
He wouldn't be flying up there

So hurrah for the men who maintain them
The oilers and grease monkeys too
Our motto and aim, Keep 'em flying
Three cheers for the army ground crew

Give us the wrench and the pliers
The will and the spirit is there
If a thing has two wings and an engine
We'll fix it to fly in the air

So hurrah for the men who maintain them
The oilers and grease monkeys too
Our motto and aim, Keep 'em flying
Three cheers for the army ground crew

Insofar as expressions are concerned, I learned one from a fellow officer later that I believe represented the sectionalism of our country fifty years ago. I believe that this was a standard expression of his, out of the mountains of North Carolina. Whenever he used it, and whenever over later years when I have found it appropriate to employ, listeners have chuckled. In describing less than perfection in someone else - especially a high ranking officer - this colleague of mine would say that the person was "more to be pitied than censured." This, of course, falls outside the bounds of popularly employed expressions that you seek; I mention it because of the sigificance that I perceive in the fact that the wartime service brought into contact persons from all over the country, tending to break down sectionalism as we came to know each other.

Anonymous

The Cot

"Leon, why ain't yu puttin' wood in the stove, I'm freezing," he shrieked in his nasal tone as he sat with his fleece-lined flying boots perched on top of a slightly warm pot belly.

"Damn you Art," bellowed Leon who was trying to nap and was rudely awakened by this outburst. "You're scheduled to be wood man tonight. Tomorrow's my turn—just look at the god-damned roster, jerk," and he rolled over angrily, pulling a rumpled G.I. woolen blanket over his fully clothed body.

Ray, the third man in this dimly lit pyramidal tent sat upright in his cot, absorbed in rereading V-letters, seemingly detached and disinterested. When the dialogue continued, he shouted, "Your lousy bickering is preventing me from concentrating on my girl friend's letters...just keep it down you two."

The verbal combatants hesitated momentarily, then in unison, shouted, "Blow it out your ass, lover boy." They laughed uproariously at their perfect unity of thought. That ended the argument, and quiet was restored.

A blast of damp English air rushed in as the flap of the tent was opened and hurriedly closed as Frank entered, still exhaling a mist of cold air and cigarette smoke. "Well guys, looks like we got a Göering's moon tonight," he said breathlessly, "We might get our midnight wake-up call from our friendly Luftwaffe, so go light on the shut-eye. If this clear weather holds up, we can finally get in some flying tomorrow."

European weather wasn't very cooperative for the air force this fall of 1943. Heavy cloud cover, intermittent fog with a chilling cold front created low morale and short tempers. This contributed to aborted missions, excessive air collisions and unacceptable losses.

The Group also had a shortage of housing. They were stationed on a hastily completed air base located on a picturesque Essex countryside, 60 miles northeast of London. The officers were housed in Quonset huts while enlisted men were billeted in 20 x 20 foot pyramidal tents, each holding six men.

In this particular tent, two cots lay naked, exposing the bare canvass. One still revealed the remnants of the previous owner's belongings; shaving lotion, toothpaste, soiled clothing, all placed haphazardly at the foot of the bed. The other had an open foot locker under the cot, empty except for some dirty socks and discarded newspapers.

Frank, looking around as he sat on his cot while removing his muddy galoshes grumbled, "Looks like you guys sure ransacked old John's stuff. Why didn't you leave me his O.D. shirt and pants? Hell, I was more his size than any of you grotesque bums."

Leon spoke up defensively, "The Headquarter boys were in here and they cleaned out the personal effects to send home. Those paper pushers knew before any of us that they never made it."

In the stillness of the darkened tent, the glow of the pot belly stove permeated this canvas enclosure with radiant warmth and serenity. Though it was a little past 10 p.m., all were dressed, absorbed in thought of home and loved ones as the lit cigarettes flitted like fireflies in the darkness. Sounds of footsteps were heard outside, and a searchlight could be seen searching for the flap of the tent. The intense beam aroused the four supine occupants who immediately were on their feet. A loud commanding voice inquired, "This tent 11? If so, this guy belongs here."

Without waiting for an answer, the voice took off, while left standing in the darkened tent was a barely visible figure. A light was put on and there stood a skinny six-foot-plus overdressed form, carrying over his stooped shoulder a barracks bag that appeared to weigh more than the person carrying it. With

an accent as southern as hominy grits, the shaky voice spoke, "S...S...'Scuse me fer barging in heah, but the Orderly people done lost ma records an ah been settin' round all day...a waitin'. Done fergit about me till a while ago...an they done sent me heah to you fellers."

Ray spoke up first, "Well rebel, grab yourself any empty cot and make yourself at home. Hope you have a long and healthy life here. By the way, what do we call you?" Before receiving an answer, Frank added, "Hey kid, looks like you just finished grammar school...bet you ain't even 18 yet."

Either ignoring or disciplined against responding to the last question, he answered, "Yup, just call me Rick...short for Richenhaus...but t'would take too durn long to explain. Mind if I sack in now...I'm sorta pooped out...been a long day." With four pair of eyes focused on the new recruit, the youngster hurriedly undressed, threw his trench coat over the bony body, and within a few minutes, was snoring soundly on the bare canvas cot.

"Damn'd if I ain't seen everything," responded Ray as he folded his letters and stuffed them in the foot locker beneath his cot. "The service must be in a bad way to allow this scrawny kid in...wonder who's ship he's assigned to...hope it ain't mine."

Frank piped in, "And what position did they place him...sure couldn't be the tail position," which evoked muffled laughter from the group. Leon, observing the lanky feet hanging over the foot of the cot remarked soberly, "Well, he took ol' Johnny's sack...hope he can get more than four missions out of that bunk...seems we already lost three this month who slept there."

At 11:15 that evening, sirens sounded a red alert, and methodically, the old veterans were already awake, putting on their warmest flying clothing. Ray commented, "Guess you were right Frank, Göering's boys are paying us a visit again tonight...more lost shut-eye."

Leon interjected, "Those damn AP's (anti-personnel bombs) are a pain in the ass...just to keep us awake and annoy the shit out of us...hope my fox-hole is dry."

(I.E. to reader. During this period of the war, Göering's air force was situated on the coast of France, just a few minutes flying time across the channel. They flew twin engine Heinkel bombers to disrupt and annoy the sleeping personnel at the air bases. Anti-personnel bombs were designed to land gently and look innocuous, shaped like rocks, butter-flies, fountain pens, flowers, and any contact would cause an explosion that would remove toes and legs, hands or inflict painful shrapnel wounds. On occasion, they would drop heavy bombs on the runways to delay operational missions or bomb and strafe aircraft. All personnel were instructed to dig individual slit trenches outside the perimeter of the air field, and remain so concealed till the green alert was sounded (all clear). Special jeeps with attached snow plow were then dispatched to clear paths around the air field and tent area to allow all personnel to return to housing. Flags were placed to guide personnel through safe areas.)

They were casually zipping up their warm clothing when Ray blurted out, "Hey guys, I can make out the sounds of those unsynchronized motors of the Heinkels, so lets get a move on, we probably got another two minutes...let's move.

As they started out the tent, someone blurted out, "We forgot the rebel...hey, he's still zonked out...get him out...quick...he's still in his underwear." The groggy freckled-faced kid finally awakened, eyes wide with fear..."Wha... what yo' all doin' to me, this some kind a joke, or in...initiation fer me...?" Art grabbed him angrily out of the cot, then shouted, "Just grab your clothes and lets go. Dress when you reach your fox hole—we got no time to explain."

The little giant just stood there petrified, then blurted, "WHAT FOX HOLE?"

"Holy shit," exclaimed Leon, "Didn't Indoctrination alert you about our Luftwaffe visitors...about digging of your own hole in the ground...?" The wailing of the sirens finally penetrated the foggy-minded recruit, and when the ground shook and ear-jarring sounds of ack-ack guns started firing, the horrified young-ster broke Art's grip, and with two long strides, was out of the tent, running like a scared rabbit, in his underwear.

Each man ran to his respective fox-hole, spaced about 100 feet apart. There were hundreds of these holes in the ground, each supporting one person. The last man to reach his hole was Leon, who was seeking the scared rabit to give him some clothing. Above the din of the guns and sirens, neighbors could see and hear his screaming to something at the top of his lungs, "Holy shit, the rebel...in my God-damned hole, get the hell out...get out...get out..." and he then tried grabbing the naked wrists of the curled up youngster...but to no avail. The kid was in a fetal position, frozen with fear and cold.

Leon gave up when the implosion of falling bombs sucked the wind out of his lungs. He made a hurried 300-yard dash for the protection of trees surrounding the air field. All eyes peering over their protective holes shouted encouragement to the ex-hausted runner. After reaching the safety of the forest, he dropped on the wet ground, mentally and physiclly exhausted.

Almost one hour later, when the all clear sounded and paths were cleared, Leon was still furious. Fuming as he walked to rejoin his buddies, he repeated over and over, "I'll kill that bastard, stupid ignoramus, should have know

better...taking my lousy fox hole. I coulda been killed, son-of-a-bitch." Approaching his fox-hole site, he observed a crowd forming. Frank hurriedly approached Leon, stopped him forcefully, then with downcast eyes and a voice shaking with emotion said, "Your hole... got a direct hit...a 250 pounder landed square one...not a bit of anything left... not even his dog tags..."

Then he added mournfully, "An' you know, we never even got his proper name." Leon looked dazed, staring blankly at this massive crater...his very own hole in the ground... All eyes were on Leon, nothing was said, but all knew what he was thinking...and feeling.

The cold pot belly cast no comforting glow in tent 11 that night. Fatigued eyes pierced the empty darkness, painfully aware of the unopened barracks bag...and empty cot.

L. Zerlin

Cartoons

THE BOWL GAZER

"Tell him to look at th' bright side of things, Willie. His trees is pruned, his ground is plowed up, an' his house is air-conditioned."

When the Lights Go On Again All Over the World

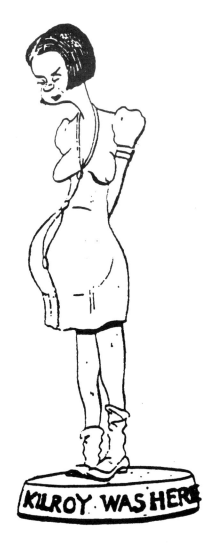

KILROY WAS HERE

"Th' hell with it, sir. Let's go back to the front."

"Them wuz his exack words—'I envy th' way you dogfaces git first pick o' wimmen an' likker in towns.'"

"Able Fox Five to Able Fox. I got a target but ya gotta be patient."

A Short Guide to
Great Britain

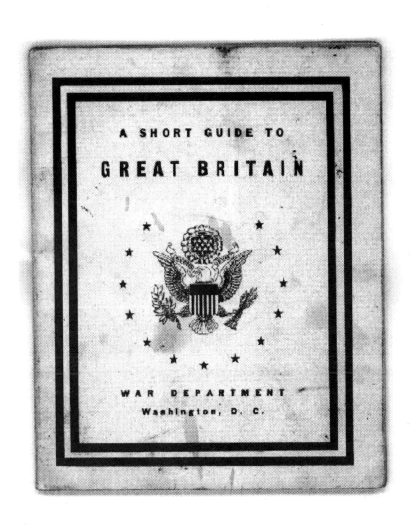

A SHORT GUIDE TO

GREAT BRITAIN

WAR DEPARTMENT
Washington, D. C.

A SHORT GUIDE TO

GREAT BRITAIN

WAR DEPARTMENT
Washington, D. C.

1

INTRODUCTION

YOU are going to Great Britain as part of an Allied offensive—to meet Hitler and beat him on his own ground. For the time being you will be Britain's guest. The purpose of this guide is to start getting you acquainted with the British, their country, and their ways.

America and Britain are allies. Hitler knows that they are both powerful countries, tough and resourceful. He knows that they, with the other United Nations, mean his crushing defeat in the end.

So it is only common sense to understand that the first and major duty Hitler has given his propaganda chiefs is to separate Britain and America and spread distrust between them. If he can do that, his chance of winning *might* return:

No Time To Fight Old Wars. If you come from an Irish-American family, you may think of the English as persecutors of the Irish, or you may think of them as enemy Redcoats who fought against us in the American Revolu-

2

tion and the War of 1812. But there is no time today to fight old wars over again or bring up old grievances. We don't worry about which side our grandfathers fought on in the Civil War, because it doesn't mean anything now.

We can defeat Hitler's propaganda with a weapon of our own. Plain, common horse sense; understanding of evident truths.

The most evident truth of all is that in their major ways of life the British and American people are much alike. They speak the same language. They both believe in representative government, in freedom of worship, in freedom of speech. But each country has minor national characteristics which differ. It is by causing misunderstanding over these minor differences that Hitler hopes to make his propaganda effective.

British Reserved, Not Unfriendly. You defeat enemy propaganda not by denying that these differences exist, but by admitting them openly and then trying to understand them. For instance: The British are often more reserved in conduct than we. On a small crowded island where forty-five million people live, each man learns to guard his privacy carefully—and is equally careful not to invade another man's privacy.

So if Britons sit in trains or busses without striking up conversation with you, it doesn't mean they are being

3

haughty and unfriendly. Probably they are paying more attention to you than you think. But they don't speak to you because they don't want to appear intrusive or rude.

Another difference. The British have phrases and colloquialisms of their own that may sound funny to you. You can make just as many boners in their eyes. It isn't a good idea, for instance, to say "bloody" in mixed company in Britain—it is one of their worst swear words. To say: "I look like a bum" is offensive to their ears, for to the British this means that you look like your own backside. It isn't important—just a tip if you are trying to shine in polite society. Near the end of this guide you will find more of these differences of speech.

British money is in pounds, shillings, and pence. (This also is explained more fully later on.) The British are used to this system and they like it, and all your arguments that the American decimal system is better won't convince them. They won't be pleased to hear you call it "funny money," either. They sweat hard to get it (wages are much lower in Britain than America) and they won't think you smart or funny for mocking at it.

Don't Be a Show Off. The British dislike bragging and showing off. American wages and American soldier's pay are the highest in the world. When pay day comes, it would be sound practice to learn to spend your money according to British standards. They consider

4

you highly paid. They won't think any better of you for throwing money around; they are more likely to feel that you haven't learned the common-sense virtues of thrift. The British "Tommy" is apt to be specially touchy about the difference between his wages and yours. Keep this in mind. Use common sense and don't rub him the wrong way.

You will find many things in Britain physically different from similar things in America. But there are also important similarities—our common speech, our common law, and our ideals of religious freedom were all brought from Britain when the Pilgrims landed at Plymouth Rock. Our ideas about political liberties are also British and parts of our own Bill of Rights were borrowed from the great charters of British liberty.

5

6

GLOSSARY OF TERMS

aisle (theatre)—*gangway*
alcohol lamp—*spirit lamp*
ale—*beer, or bitter*
apartment—*flat*
apartment house—*block of flats*
ash can—*dust bin*
ashman—*dustman*
atomizer—*scent spray*
automobile—*motor car, or car*
baby carriage—*perambulator, or pram*
baggage—*luggage*
baggage car—*luggage van*
bakery—*baker's shop*
bathrobe—*dressing gown*
bartender—*barman, or potman*
bathtub—*bath*
battery (automobile)—*accumulator*
beach—*seaside*
beer—*lager*
bill (money)—*banknote, or note*
billboard—*hoarding*
biscuit—*scone, or tea cake*
bouncer—*chucker out*
bowling alley—*skittle alley*
broiled (meat)—*grilled*
business suit—*lounge suit*
call up—*ring up*
candy (hard)—*boiled sweets*

candy store—*sweet shop*
cane—*stick*
can opener—*tin opener, or key*
carom (billiards)—*cannon*
chain store—*multiple shop*
check baggage—*register luggage*
checkers (game)—*draughts*
chickenyard—*fowl run*
cigarette butt—*cigarette end*
closed season (for game)—*close season*
conductor—*guard*
closet—*cupboard*
coal oil—*paraffin*
collar button—*collar stud*
cookie—*biscuit*
cop—*bobby*
corn—*maize, or Indian corn*
cornmeal—*Indian meal*
cotton (absorbent)—*cotton wool*
cracker—*biscuit (unsweetened)*
daylight-saving time—*summer time*
deck (of cards)—*pack*
derby (hat)—*bowler, or hard hat*
dessert—*sweet*
dishpan—*washing-up bowl*
drawers (men's)—*pants*
druggist—*chemist*

drug store—*chemist's shop*
drygoods store—*draper's shop*
elevator—*lift*
fender (automobile)—*wing, or mudguard*
fish dealer—*fishmonger*
five-and-ten (store)—*bazaar*
floorwalker—*shopwalker*
frame house—*wooden house*
fruit seller (or dealer)—*fruiterer*
fruit store—*fruiterer's*
fresh fruit—*dessert (at the end of a meal)*
french fried potatoes—*chips*
freight car—*goods wagon*
garters (men's)—*sock suspenders*
gasoline, or gas—*petrol*
gear shift (automobile)—*gear lever*
generator (automobile) — *dynamo*
ground wire (radio)—*earth wire*
guy—*bloke, fellow*
haberdashery—*men's wear*
hardware—*ironmongery*
headliner (vaudeville)—*topliner*
highball—*whiskey and soda*
hood (automobile)—*bonnet*
huckster—*coster, or hawker*
hunting—*shooting*
ill, sick—*ill, queer*
instalment plan—*hire-purchase system, or hire system*
intermission—*interval*
janitor—*caretaker, or porter*
junk—*rubbish*

lawyer—*solicitor*
legal holiday—*bank holiday*
line up—*queue up*
living room—*sitting room*
lobby (theatre)—*foyer, or entrance hall*
long distance (telephone)—*trunks*
low gear (automobile)—*first speed*
mail a letter—*post a letter*
mail box—*pillar box*
marriage certificate—*marriage lines*
molasses—*black treacle*
monkey wrench—*screw spanner*
movie house—*cinema*
movies—*flicks*
mucilage—*gum*
muffler (automobile)—*silencer*
necktie—*tie*
newsstand—*kiosk*
oatmeal (boiled)—*porridge*
oil pan (automobile)—*sump*
okay—*righto*
orchestra seats—*stalls*
package—*parcel*
pebbly beach—*shingle*
phonograph—*gramophone*
pie (fruit)—*tart*
pitcher—*jug*
poolroom—*billiards saloon*
potato chips—*crisps*
private hospital—*nursing home*
push cart—*barrow*
race track—*race course*

7

radio—*wireless*
railway car—*railway carriage*
raincoat—*mackintosh, or mac, or waterproof*
roadster (automobile) — *two-seater*
roast (of meat)—*joint*
roller coaster—*switchback-railway*
rolling grasslands—*downs*
round trip—*return trip*
roomer—*lodger*
rooster—*cock, or cockerel*
rubbers—*galoshes*
rumble seat—*dickey*
run (in a stocking)—*ladder*
saloon—*public house, or pub*
scallion—*spring onion*
scrambled eggs—*buttered eggs*
second floor—*first floor*
sedan (automobile)—*saloon car*
sewerage (house)—*drains*
shoestring—*bootlace, or shoelace*
shot (athletics)—*weight*
shoulder (of road)—*verge*
rubberneck wagon—*char-a-banc*
silverware—*plate*
slacks—*bags*
sled—*sledge*
smoked herring—*kipper*
soda biscuit (or cracker)—*cream-cracker*
soft drinks—*minerals*
spark plug—*sparking-plug*
spigot (or faucet)—*tap*
squash—*vegetable marrow*

stairway—*staircase, or stairs*
string bean—*French-bean*
store—*shop*
subway—*underground*
sugar-bowl—*sugar-basin*
suspenders (men's)—*braces*
sweater—*pull-over*
syrup—*treacle*
taffy—*toffee*
taxi stand—*cab rank*
telegram—*wire*
tenderloin (of beef)—*under-cut, or fillet*
ten pins—*nine pins*
thumb-tack—*drawing pin*
ticket office—*booking office*
toilet—*lavatory, closet*
top (automobile)—*hood*
transom (of door)—*fanlight*
trolley—*tram*
truck—*lorry*
undershirt—*vest, or singlet*
union-suit—*combinations*
vaudeville—*variety*
vaudeville theatre—*music hall*
vest—*waistcoat*
vomit—*be sick*
washbowl—*washbasin*
washrag—*face cloth*
washstand—*wash-hand stand*
water heater—*geyser*
window shade—*blind*
"you're connected"—"you're through" (telephone)
windshield (automobile)—*windscreen*

8

TABLE OF BRITISH CURRENCY

Copper Coins

Symbol	Name	British value	American value (approximate)
¼d.	farthing (rare)	¼ penny	½ cent.
½d.	halfpenny ("hay-p'ny")	½ penny	1 cent.
1d.	penny	1 penny	2 cents.
3d.	threepence ("thrup- pence" or "thrup- 'ny bit"; rare).	3 pence	5 cents.

Silver Coins

3d.	threepence ("thrup- pence" or "thrup- 'ny bit"; not com- mon in cities).	3 pence	5 cents.
6d.	sixpence	6 pence	10 cents.
1s.	shilling (or "bob")	12 pence	20 cents.
2s.	florin (fairly rare)	2 shillings	40 cents.
2s. 6d.	half crown (or "two and six").	2½ shillings	50 cents.
5s.	crown (rare)	5 shillings	$1.00.

Paper Currency

10s.	10-shilling note	10 shillings (or ½ pound).	$2.00
1	pound note	20 shillings	$4.00.
5	5-pound note	5 pounds	$20.00.

9

The British Came Through. For many months the people of Britain have been doing without things which Americans take for granted. But you will find that shortages, dis- comforts, blackouts, and bombings have not made the British depressed. They have a new cheerfulness and a new determination born out of hard times and tough luck. After going through what they have been through it's only human nature that they should be more than ever determined to win.

You are coming to Britain from a country where your home is still safe, food is still plentiful, and lights are still burning. So it is doubly important for you to remem- ber that the British soldiers and civilians have been living under a tremendous strain. It is always impolite to criti- cize your hosts. It is militarily stupid to insult your allies. So stop and think before you sound off about luke- warm beer, or cold boiled potatoes, or the way English cigarettes taste.

If British civilians look dowdy and badly dressed, it is not because they do not like good clothes or know how to wear them. All clothing is rationed and the British know that they help war production by wearing an old suit or dress until it cannot be patched any longer. Old clothes are "good form."

10

One thing to be careful about—if you are invited into a British home and the host exhorts you to "eat up— there's plenty on the table," go easy. It may be the fam- ily's rations for a whole week spread out to show their hospitality.

Waste Means Lives. It is always said that Americans throw more food into their garbage cans than any other country eats. It is true. We have always been a "pro- ducer" nation. Most British food is imported even in peacetimes, and for the last two years the British have been taught not to waste the things that their ships bring in from abroad. British seamen die getting those convoys through. The British have been taught this so thoroughly that they now know that gasoline and food represent the lives of merchant sailors. And when you burn gasoline needlessly, it will seem to them as if you are wasting the blood of those seamen—when you destroy or waste food you have wasted the life of another sailor.

British Women At War. A British woman officer or non- commissioned officer can—and often does—give orders to a man private. The men obey smartly and know it is no shame. For British women have proven themselves in this war. They have stuck to their posts near burning ammu- nition dumps, delivered messages afoot after their motor- cycles have been blasted from under them. They have pulled aviators from burning planes. They have died at

11

the gun posts and as they fell another girl has stepped directly into the position and "carried on." There is not a *single record* in this war of any British woman in uni- formed service quitting her post or failing in her duty under fire.

Now you understand why British soldiers respect the women in uniform. They have won the right to the utmost respect. When you see a girl in khaki or air-force blue with a bit of ribbon on her tunic—remember she didn't get it for knitting more socks than anyone else in Ipswich.

12

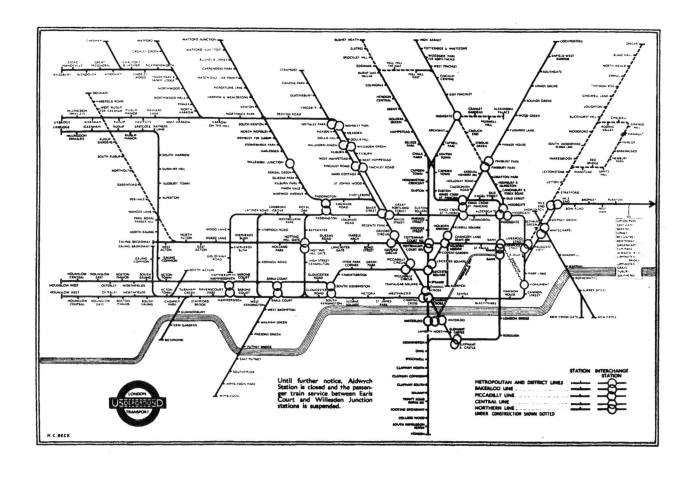

Until further notice, Aldwych Station is closed and the passenger train service between Earls Court and Willesden Junction stations is suspended.

H.C. BECK

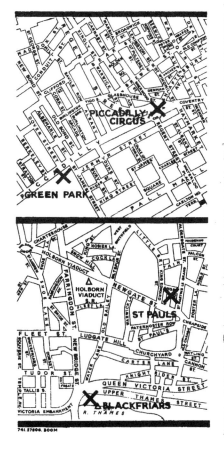

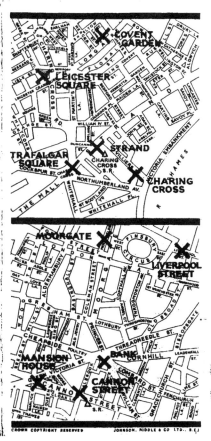

UNDERGROUND LINES

Number 2 1941

ISSUED FREE

LONDON TRANSPORT
55 BROADWAY SW1 ABBey 1234

WWII
by the Numbers

• Aircraft Strength • Military Manpower • Tons Bombs Dropped •
Sorties Flown • Marine Corps Squadrons • Naval Strengths of
Combatants • Major Naval Engagements • Military and Civilian
Casualties • Ground Force Casualties • Naval Losses...U.S. and
Japanese • Types of Aircraft and Specifications • Fastest Fighter
Planes • Air Force Losses • V1 and V2 specifications • Aces of the
War • Aircraft Strength • Military Manpower • Tons Bombs
Dropped • Sorties Flown • Marine Corps Squadrons •
Naval Strengths of Combatants • Major
Naval Engagements • Military and
Civilian Casualties • Ground Force
Casualties • Naval Losses...U.S. and
Japanese • Types of Aircraft and
Specifications • Fastest Fighter Planes •
Air Force Losses • V1 and V2
specifications • Aces of the War •
Aircraft Strength • Military Manpower •
Tons Bombs Dropped • Sorties Flown •
Marine Corps Squadrons • Naval
Strengths of Combatants • Major Naval
Engagements • Military and Civilian
Casualties • Ground Force Casualties •
Naval Losses...U.S. and Japanese •
Types of Aircraft and Specifications •
Fastest Fighter Planes • Air Force
Losses • V1 and V2 specifications • Aces
of the War • Aircraft Strength • Military
Manpower • Tons Bombs Dropped •
Sorties Flown • Marine Corps Squadrons
• Naval Strengths of Combatants • Major
Naval Engagements • Military and
Civilian Casualties • Ground Force
Casualties • Naval Losses...U.S. and
Japanese • Types of Aircraft and
Specifications • Fastest Fighter Planes
• Air Force Losses • V1 and V2
specifications • Aces of the War •
Aircraft Strength • Military
Manpower • Tons Bombs Dropped
• Sorties Flown • Marine Corps
Squadrons • Naval Strengths of
Combatants • Major Naval
Engagements • Military and
Civilian Casualties •
Ground Force
Casualties • Naval
Losses...U.S.
a n d

The Leading Fighter Pilots, All Nations

To earn the distinction of being an ace a pilot had to score a minimum of five "kills," or victories. As difficult as that was, the list of all the aces would fill several pages (there were 330 in the U.S. Navy alone). Those listed here are aces who earned the title *five times over or more*, meaning a minimum of twenty-five "kills." In addition, thirty-eight German fighter Aces *scored over 100 "kills,"* making them the unchallenged super aces of the war. In the interest of brevity, only German super aces with more than 250 kills each have been listed.

Fighter Ace/Nationality	*Number of Kills*
Erich Hartmann, Germany	352
Gerhard Barkhorn, Germany	301
Gunther Rall, Germany	275
Otto Kittel, Germany	267
Walther Nowotny, Germany	255
Hiroyishi Nishizawa, Japan	87*
Shoichi Sugita, Japan	80*
Hans H. Wind, Finland	75
Saburo Sakai, Japan	64†
Ivan Kozhedub, Russia	62
Aleksandr Pokryshkin, Russia	59
Grigorii Rechkalov, Russia	58
Hiromichi Shinohara, Japan	58
Nikolai Gulaev, Russia	57
Waturo Nakamichi, Japan	55
Takeo Okumura, Japan	54
Naoshi Kanno, Japan	52
Kirill Yevstigneev, Russia	52
Satoshi Anabuki, Japan	51
Yasuhiko Kuroe, Japan	51
Dimitrii Glinka, Russia	50
Aleksandr Klubov, Russia	50
Ivan Pilipenko, Russia	48
Arsenii Vorozheikin, Russia	46
Vasilii Kubarev, Russia	46
Nikolai Skomorokhov, Russia	46
J. Pattle, South Africa	41
Richard I. Bong, U.S.A.	40
Thomas B. McGuire, U.S.A.	38
J. E. Johnson, Great Britain	38
A. G. Malan, South Africa	35
David McCampbell, U.S.A.	34
P. H. Closterman, France	33
B. Finucane, Ireland	32

*Some works credit Shoichi Sugita with 120 kills and Nishizawa with 103.

†Saburo Sakai has been credited with 80 kills in another work. (Though this author is satisfied that the figures given here are correct, the discrepancies have been pointed out because they do exist.)

Fighter Ace/Nationality	Number of Kills
G. F. Beurling, Canada	31⅓
Frances S. Gabreski, U.S.A.	31
J. R. D. Graham, Great Britain	29
R. R. S. Tuck, Great Britain	29
C. R. Caldwell, Australia	28½
Gregory Boyington, U.S.A.	28
J. Frantisek, Czechoslovakia	28
Robert S. Johnson, U.S.A.	28
J. H. Lacey, Great Britain	28
C. F. Gray, New Zealand	27½
Charles H. MacDonald, U.S.A.	27
George E. Preddy, U.S.A.	26
E. S. Lock, Great Britain	26
Joseph J. Foss, U.S.A.	26
Robert M. Hanson, U.S.A.	25

The Fastest Fighter Planes of the War

There were sixty-four different versions of fighter planes, land-based and carrier-borne, produced by Allied and Axis powers during the war. In addition, there were fighter-bombers. Below are the nineteen fastest fighters that had maximum speeds over 400 miles per hour.

Plane/Country	Maximum Speed	Maximum Range
Messerschmitt Me-263, Germany	596 mph (rocket)	N.A.
Messerschmitt Me-262, Germany	560 mph (jet)	650 miles
Heinkel He-162A, Germany	553 mph	606 miles
P-51-H, United States	487 mph	850 miles
Lavochkin La-11, Russia	460 mph	466 miles
Spitfire XIV, Great Britain	448 mph	460 miles
Yakovlev Yak-3, Russia	447 mph	506 miles
P-51-D Mustang, United States	440 mph	2,300 miles
Tempest VI, Great Britain	438 mph	740 miles
Focke-Wulf FW-190D, Germany	435 mph	560 miles
Lavochkin 9, Russia	429 mph	1,078 miles
P-47-D Thunderbolt, United States	428 mph	1,000 miles
Lavochkin La-7, Russia	423 mph	392 miles
F4U Corsair, United States	417 mph	1,015 miles
Yakovlev Yak-9P, Russia	416 mph	889 miles
P-38-L Lightning, United States	414 mph	460 miles
Typhoon, Great Britain	412 mph	510 miles
Lavochkin La-5FN, Russia	401 mph	528 miles
Messerschmitt Me-109G, Germany	400 mph	460 miles

FACTS: AIRBORNE DIVISIONS

1st Abn. Div. Fought at Leyte, Cavite, and Manila

13th Abn. Div. Only airborne division not to see action in WWII

17th Abn. Div. Fought at the Rhine Crossing and in Germany

82nd Abn. Div. Fought in Sicily, Italy, Normandy, Ardennes, and Nijmegen.

101st. Abn. Div. Fought in Normandy and Battle of the Bulge.

U.S. airborne were the world's only paratroopers with reserve 'chutes.

AMERICA'S TOP TWENTY ACES OF WORLD WAR II

Richard Bong - 40

Thomas B. McGuire - 38

David M. Campbell - 34

Francis S. Gabreski - 28

Gregory Boyington - 28

Robert S. Johnson - 28

Charles H. MacDonald - 27

Joseph J. Foss - 26

George E. Preddy 25.83

Robert M. Hanson - 25

John C. Meyers - 24

Cecil E. Harris - 24

Eugene A. Balencia - 23

Raymond S. Wetmore - 22.6

David S. Schilling - 22.5

Gerald R. Johnson - 22

Neel E. Kearby - 22

Jay T. Robbins - 22

Don S. Gentile - 21.84

Fredrick J. Christiansen - 21.5

U.S. ARMIES

First Army	General Omar Bradley	fought in France and Germany
Third Army	Gen. George S. Patton	fought in France and Germany
Fourth Army	Remained Stateside	
Fifth Army	Gen. Mark Clark	fought in Italy
Sixth Army	Gen. Walter Krueger	fought in so. France and Germany
Seventh Army	Gen. Alex. Patch	fought in so. France and Germany
Eighth Army	Gen. Robt. Eichenlberger	fought in the Philippines
Ninth Army	Gen. Wm. H. Simpson	fought in France and Germany
Tenth Army	Gen. Simon Buckner	fought in Okinawa

U.S. AIRCRAFT CARRIER DESIGNATIONS

CV aircraft carrier

CVA attack aircraft carrier

CVB large aircraft carrier

CVL small aircraft carrier

CVE escort aircraft carrier

CVS seaplane aircraft carrier

U.S. ARMY AIR FORCES

First Air Force	Northeast Air District contintental U.S.
Second Air Force	Northeast Air District continental U.S.
Third Air Force	Southeast Air District contintental U.S.
Fourth Air Force	Southeast Air District contintental U.S
Fifth Air Force	Southwest Pacific
Sixth Air Force	Panama Canal Zone and Caribbean
Seventh Air Force	Central Pacific
Eighth Air Force	England
Ninth Air Force	North Africa and England
Tenth Air Force	India and Burma
Eleventh Air Force	Aleutian Islands and Northern Pacific
Twelfth Air Force	North Africa
Thirteenth Air Force	Southwest Pacific
Fourteenth Air Force	China (formerly American Volunteer Group, AVG)
Fifteenth Air Force	Italy
Twentieth Air Force	Japan(B-29s)

ARMY ORGANIZATIONS

UNIT	COMPOSITION	IN CHARGE
squad	8 to 12 men	sergeant
platoon	3 or more squads	lieutenant
company	3 or more platoons	captain
battalion	3 or more companies	lieutenant colonel
regiment	3 or more battalions	colonel
brigade	3 or more regiments	brigadier general
division	3 or more brigades	major general
corps	3 or more divisions	lieutenant general
army	3 or more corps	general
army group	3 or more armies	general or field marshal

U.S. CARRIERS AT BEGINNING OF WAR

Langley (CV-1)

Lexington (CV-2)

Saratoga (CV-3)

Ranger (CV-4)

Yorktown (CV-5)

Enterprise (CV-6)

Wasp (CV-7)

Hornet (CV-8)

The U.S. had over 100 aircraft carriers at the end of the war.

CODE NAMES

Alamo . . . . U.S. Sixth Army

Conquer . . . . . U.S. Ninth Army

Eagle . . . . U.S. Twelfth Army Group

Lion . . . . British Twenty-first Army Group

Lucky . . . . U.S. Third Army

Master . . . . U.S. First Army

Shellburst . . . . . Supreme Headquarters
American Expeditionary Force

Speedy . . . . . . U.S. Second Corps

U.S. NAVY - LANDING CRAFT DESIGNATIONS

LCA . . . . . landing craft, assault

LCC . . . . . landing craft, control

LCF . . . . . landing craft, flak

LC . . . . . . landing craft, flotilla flagship

LCI . . . . . landing craft, infantry

LCM . . . . landing craft, mechanized

LCP . . . . . landing craft, personnel

LCR . . . . landing craft, rubber

LCS . . . . landing craft, support

LCS . . . . landing craft, small support

LCT . . . . landing craft, tank

LCTR . . . . landing craft, tank (rocket)

LCV . . . . landing craft, vehicle

LCVP . . . landing craft, vehicle, personnel

LSD . . . . landing ship, dock

LSM . . . . landing ship, medium

LSMR . . . . landing ship, medium (rocket)

LST . . . . (H) landing ship, tank (hospital)

LSV . . . . landing vehicle, tracked

U.S. NAVY AIRCRAFT NAMES

Hellcat . . . . . F6F Fighter

Wildcat F4F

Corsair F4U

Tigercat . . . F7F

Helldiver . . . SB2C Scout Bomber

Dauntless . . SBD

Devastator . TSD Torpedo Bomber

Avenger . . . . TFB/TBM

Seahawk . . . SC, Scout Observation Float Plane

Seagull . . . . SOC

Kingfisher . . OS2U

Sentinel . . . OY-1, Land Based Liaison (L-2)

Privateer . . . PB4Y-2, Land Based Patrol Bomber

Ventura . . . . PV-1, Land Based Patrol Bomber

Nomad . . . . PBN, Flying Boat

Catalina . . . PBY, Flying Boat

Coronado . . PB2Y

Mariner . . . . PBM, Flying Boat

AIR FORCE AIRCRAFT

Lightning. P38
Flying Fortress B17
Flying Tiger P40
Thunderbolt P47

Mitchell B25
Liberator B24
Marauder B26
Mustang P51

SHIPS BUILT FROM JULY 1, 1940 THROUGH AUGUST 31, 1945

Battleships - 10
Aircraft Carriers - (CV, CVL) - 27
Escort Carriers - (CVE) - 111
Cruisers - (CB, CA, CL) - 47
Destroyers - 370
Destroyer Escorts - 504
Submarines - 217

Minecraft - 975
Patrol Ships and Craft - 1,915
Auxiliary Ships - 1612
Landing Ships and Craft - 66,055
District Craft (Yard Craft) - 3,053

TOTAL......74,896

DRAFT CLASSIFICATIONS

1A   fit for military service
1B   fit for limited military service
1C   member of the armed forces
1D   student fit for general military service
1E   student fit for limited military service
2A   deferred for critical civilian work

3A   deferred
4A   already served in the armed services
4B   deferred by law, i.e., draft officials
4C   alien
4D   minister
4E   conscientious objector
4F   physically, mentally or morally unfit

BATTLESHIPS STATIONED AT PEARL HARBOR DURING ATTACK

U.S.S. Arizona - sunk
U.S.S. California - sunk but salvaged
U.S.S. Maryland - damaged
U.S.S. Nevada - beached but salvaged
U.S.S. Oklahoma - sunk

U.S.S. Pennsylvania - damaged
U.S.S. Tennessee - damaged
U.S.S. Utah - sunk
U.S.S. West Virginia - sunk but salvaged

CONCENTRATION CAMPS OF WWII

Auschwitz
Belzec
Belsen
Buchenwald
Chelmno

Dachau
Flossenburg
Mauthausen
Oranienburg
Ravensbruck

Sachsenhausen
Sobibor
Theresienstadt
Treblinka

NUREMBURG – DEFENDANTS' SENTENCES

Herman Goering	death - committed suicide
Joachim von Ribbentrop	death
Wilheim Keitel	death
Ernst Kaltenbrunner	death
Alfred Rosenberg	death
Hans Frank	death
Wilhelm Frick	death
Julius Saukel	death
Fritz Saukel	death
Alfred Jodl	death
Arthus Seyss	death
Rudolph Hess	life imprisonment
Walter Funk	life imprisonment
Eric Raeder	life imprisonment
Baldur von Schirach	twenty years
Albert Speer	twenty years
Constantin von Neurath	fifteen years
Karl Doenitz	ten years
Hjalmar Schacht	acquitted
Franz von Papen	acquitted
Han Fritzsche	acquitted
Robert Ley	committed suicide awaiting trial
Martin Borman	death in abstentia

AIRCRAFT NAMED FOR FAMOUS PEOPLE

General Harold Alexander.......... Patches C-47

General Omar Bradley............. Mary Q C-47

General George Brett .... Swoose B-17

Winston Churchil .... Commando LB-30

Charles de Gaulle .... France C-56

General Ira C. Eaker .... Yankee Doodle B-17

General Toy S. Geiger .... Blue Goose .... PBY

General George Kenney .... Sally............. B-17

General Douglas MacArthur .... Bataan B-17

Field Marshal Montgomery .... #19082.............. B-17

Elliott Roosevelt .... Jingle Jangle B-17

President Franklin Roosevelt .... Sacred Cow C-87

President Harry Truman .... Independence.......... C-87

Wendell Wilkie .... Gulliver............. C-87

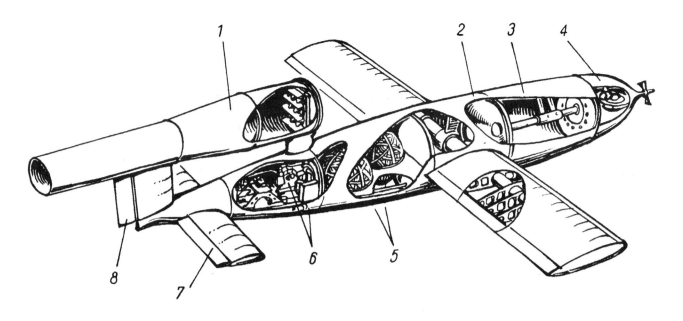

3. The V-1
1. pulse-jet engine *2.* fuel tank *3.* warhead *4.* magnetic compass *5.* compressed air tanks *6.* batteries *7.* altitude vanes *8.* direction vanes

Figures concerning the V-1 and V-2 during the Second World War

	V-1	**V-2**
Produced	30,000-32,000	c. 6,000 (half for trials)
Fired operationally	20,000	c. 3,000
Against London	10,492 (7,488 reached England; 2,420 fell on target)	c. 1,300 (517 fell on target)
Against other cities in Great Britain	3,132	537 (61 fell into the sea)
Against Antwerp	2,448 (not all exploded)	1,265 (some fell in the vicinity)
Against Brussels and other towns	not known	447
Against the whole of Belgium	6,585 (RAF and A-A shot down 2,455)	as above
Against Paris	none	19
Against other cities	Antwerp 1,800 Liège 1,096	Norwich 43, Liège 27, Lille 25, Tourcoing 19, Maastricht 19, Hasselt 13, Tournai 9, Arras 6, Cambrai 4, Mons 3, Diest 2, Ipswich 1
Number of people killed in Great Britain	5,864	London 2,511 other places 213
Wounded in Great Britain	badly 17,197 lightly 23,174	London 5,869 other places 598

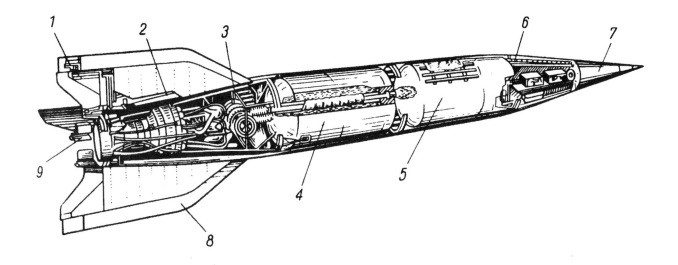

4. The V-2
1. external vanes 2. rocket motor 3. pumps 4. oxygen tank 5. alcohol tank 6. automatic pilot 7. warhead 8. stabilizers 9. graphite vanes

	V-1	**V-2**
Number of people killed on the Continent	Antwerp (V-1 and V-2 combined) The vicinity (V-1 and V-2 combined)	2,915 895
Wounded on the Continent	Antwerp (V-1 and V-2 combined) The vicinity (V-1 and V-2 combined)	4,810 1,264
Houses destroyed in Great Britain	24,491	5,000
Houses damaged in Great Britain	badly 52,293 lightly 50,000	as above
Houses destroyed in Antwerp and the vicinity	(V-1 and V-2 combined)	3,613
Houses damaged in Antwerp and the vicinity	(V-1 and V-2 combined)	badly 29,352 lightly 77,322

The V-1 offensive against London lasted from 13 June 1944 to 29 March 1945, and against Antwerp from October 1944 to 29 March 1945. The V-2 offensive against London lasted from 8 September 1944 to 27 March 1945 and against Antwerp from October 1944 to 27 March 1945.

The British and American Air Forces, between August 1943 and March 1945, carried out 68,913 individual sorties and dropped 122,133 tons of bombs on all targets directly connected with V-weapons, of which 98,000 tons fell on targets connected solely with the V-1.

The British defence against the V-1 shot down or destroyed 3,957 of them in the following manner: fighters, 1,847; A-A, 1,878; barrage balloons, 232.

World War II Statistics

- Military Manpower of all Billigerents, 1939-1945
- Tank Strengths of Panzer Divisions
- German and Allied Aircraft, 1938-1945
- Tons Bombs Dropped and Sorties Flown, 1942-1945
- Total U.S. Marine Corps Squadrons
- Sorties Flown in Pacific by U.S. Forces, 1941-1945
- Naval Strengths of all nations on Entry into War
- Military and Civilian Casualties, 1939-1945
- Army Battle Casualties in Major Campaigns, 1939-1945
- British and 8th U.S. Air Force Losses, 1939-1945
- Combat and Non-Combat Injuries and Diseases, 1939-1945
- Naval Losses of Major Belligerents, 1939-1945
- Production of Military Trucks and Lorries, 1939–1945
- Annual Allied and Axis production of Aircraft, 1939-1945
- Fighters and Ground Attack Aircraft
- Dive and Torpedo Bombers and Ground Attack
- Bombers of All Nations

PART I MILITARY MANPOWER

The three tables following deal mainly with the ground forces of the Second World War belligerents, though air force and naval personnel strengths are also given for those countries which had significant such arms. Table 9 gives details on all the countries involved, whilst the following table lists selected countries and shows what proportion of their ground forces actually served overseas. (Air forces and navies are too mobile to allow this kind of distinction to be made.) Where possible this table also distinguishes between the theatres to which the soldiers were posted. With this latter point in mind, Table 11 deals with Germany only and attempts to compute the military effort expended on the Eastern Front as opposed to the other theatres.

The following points should be borne in mind when consulting these tables:
— In Table 9, especially, the data given for certain countries can only be an informed approximation.
— The overall figures for ground forces given below are not an accurate reflection of the number of men actually in the firing line. This figure, both for the war as a whole or for an individual campaign, is best arrived at by combining the data on divisions in the Orders of Battle and the Tables of Organisation and Equipment sections.
— Where a dash is given in Table 9 it indicates that the figure for that column is not significantly different from that in the previous completed column.

Table 9 Military Manpower Raised, by Each of the Belligerent Nations, 1939-45

COUNTRY		ON ENTRY INTO WAR	END OF WAR	PEAK NUMBER *	TOTAL MOBILISED †
Albania		13,000	—	—	—
Australia	Armed Forces	91,700	575,100	—	993,000
	Army	82,800	380,700	—	727,200
	Air Force	3,500	154,500	—	216,900
	Navy	5,400	39,900	—	48,900
Belgium		600,000	650,000	—	(900,000)
Bulgaria		160,000 ‡	450,000 (with Soviets)	—	1,011,000
Canada	Armed Forces	63,100	759,800	—	1,100,000
	Army	55,600	474,000	—	690,000
	Air Force	3,100	193,000	—	222,500
	Navy	4,400	92,800	—	99,400
China		2,500,000 (1937)	5,000,000	5,700,000	14,000,000
Denmark		6,600	—	—	—
Finland	1939-40	127,800	200,000	—	?
	1941-44	400,000	270,000	—	?
France	Sept 1939	900,000	—	—	—
	1940	2,680,000 ††	—	—	—
	1943-44 Italy	15,000	98,000	113,000	160,000
	1944-45 N.W.E.	?	437,000	—	?
Germany	Armed Forces	3,180,000	7,800,000	9,500,000	17,900,000
	△ Army	2,730,000 (30,000)	6,100,000 (800,000)	6,500,000	?
	Air Force	400,000	1,000,000 **	2,100,000	?
	Navy	50,000	700,000	800,000	?
Greece	Oct 1940	430,000	—	—	?
	April 1941	540,000	—	—	?
Hungary		80,000 (1939)	210,000	?	?
India	Armed Forces	197,000	2,159,700	—	2,581,800
	Army	194,900	2,100,000	—	2,500,000
	Air Force	300	29,200	—	52,800
	Navy	1,800	30,500	—	29,000

* Only given when significantly different from preceding columns.

† Numbers in brackets denote theoretical figure.

‡ Active Army only.

†† There were also 1,640,000 men in the Army of the Interior.

△ Figures in brackets are Waffen-SS numbers.

** Some sources give between 1.5 million and 1.8 million.

Table 9 Military Manpower Raised, by Each of the Belligerent Nations, 1939-45 continued

COUNTRY		ON ENTRY INTO WAR	END OF WAR	PEAK NUMBER *	TOTAL MOBILISED †
Italy	Armed Forces	1,899,600	?	?	9,100,000
	Army	1,630,000	?	2,563,000	?
	Air Force	101,000	(May 43) 200,000	—	?
	Navy	168,600	(Sept 43) 259,100	—	?
Japan	Armed Forces	1,700,000	7,200,000	—	9,100,000
	Army	1,500,000	5,500,000	—	?
	Navy	200,000	1,700,000	—	?
Netherlands		270,000	400,000	—	400,000
New Zealand	Armed Forces	13,800	192,800	—	?
	Army	11,300	157,000	—	?
	Air Force	1,200	c. 27,000	—	?
	Navy	1,300	5,800	—	?
Norway		25,000	—	—	(90,000)
Poland	1939	1,200,000	250,000	?	(2,400,000)
	1943-45 Italy	8,600	50,000	—	?
	1944-45 N.W.E.	28,000	—	—	?
	1941-45 E.Front	30,000	?	?	200,000
Rumania	1941-44	686,000	1,225,000	—	?
	1944-45 with Red Army	?	370,000	—	539,000
S.Africa	Armed Forces	?	?	?	250,000
	Army	18,000	?	198,000	208,000
	Air Force	1,000	?	?	38,000
	Navy	?	?	?	4,000
UK	Armed Forces	681,000	4,683,000	—	5,896,000
	Army	402,000	2,931,000	—	3,778,000
	Air Force	118,000	963,000	1,012,000	1,185,000
	Navy	161,000	789,000	—	923,000
USA	Armed Forces	5,413,000	11,877,000	—	16,354,000
	†† Army	4,602,000	5,851,000	—	} 11,260,000
	Air Force	354,000	2,282,000	—	
	Navy	382,000	3,288,000	—	4,183,000
	US M.C.	75,000	456,000	—	669,000
USSR	Armed Forces	9,000,000	12,400,000	13,200,000	?
	‡‡ Army	2,900,000	6,000,000	—	?
	Air Force	?	?	?	?
	Navy	?	?	266,000	?
Yugoslavia	1941	150,000	?	—	(1,500,000)
	1941-45 Partisans	(Dec) 2,000	800,000	—	?

* Only given when significantly different from preceding columns.

† Numbers in brackets denote theoretical figure.

†† Not including USAAF.

‡‡ With army groups on the German front. German sources give a figure in excess of 4.5 million for June 1941.

Table 23 Tons Bombs Dropped and Sorties Flown by the Allied Air Forces in Europe August 1942-May 1945

DATE 1942	BOMBER COMMAND		8 US AIR FORCE		15 US AIR FORCE		BALKAN AIR FORCE	
	TONS DROPPED	NUMBER* SORTIES	TONS DROPPED	NUMBER SORTIES	TONS DROPPED	NUMBER SORTIES	TONS DROPPED	NUMBER† SORTIES
August	4,162	2,454 186	151	114	—	—	—	—
September	5,595	3,489 127	188	183	—	—	—	—
October	3,809	2,198 406	278	284	—	—	—	—
November	2,423	2,067 127	604	519	—	—	—	—
December	2,714	1,758 200	340	353	—	—	—	—
TOTAL	**18,703**	**11,966 1,046**	**1,411**	**1,453**	—	—	—	—
1943								
January	4,345	2,556 406	594	338	—	—	—	—
February	10,959	5,030 426	568	526	—	—	—	—
March	10,591	5,174 284	1,483	956	—	—	—	—
April	11,467	5,571 316	858	449	—	—	—	—
May	12,290	5,130 360	2,555	1,672	—	—	—	—
June	15,271	5,816 —	2,330	2,107	—	—	—	—
July	16,830	6,170 —	3,475	2,829	—	—	—	—
August	20,149	7,807 —	3,999	2,265	—	—	—	—
September	14,855	5,513 —	7,369	3,259	—	—	—	—
October	13,773	4,638 —	4,548	2,831	—	—	—	—
November	14,495	5,208 —	5,751	4,157	5,392	1,785	—	—
December	11,802	4,123 —	10,655	5,973	7,752	2,039	—	—
TOTAL	**157,367**	**62,736 1,792**	**44,185**	**27,362**	**13,144**	**3,824**	—	—
1944								
January	18,428	6,278 —	10,532	6,367	11,051	4,720	—	—
February	12,054	4,263 45	16,480	9,884	6,747	3,981	—	—
March	27,698	9,031 18	19,892	11,590	10,176	5,996	—	—
April	33,496	9,873 10	22,447	14,464	21,256	10,182	—	—
May	37,252	11,353 16	32,450	19,825	30,355	14,432	—	—
June	57,267	13,592 2,371	54,204	28,925	27,466	11,761	—	—
July	57,615	11,500 6,298	40,784	23,917	32,183	12,642	132	2,509

* The top figure for each month is night sorties, the bottom day.

† All types aircraft.

Table 23 Tons Bombs Dropped and Sorties Flown by Allied Air Forces in Europe August 1942-May 1945 (continued)

* The top figure for each month is night sorties, the bottom day.

† All types aircraft.

DATE 1944	BOMBER COMMAND		8 US AIR FORCE		15 US AIR FORCE		BALKAN AIR FORCE	
	TONS DROPPED	NUMBER* SORTIES	TONS DROPPED	NUMBER SORTIES	TONS DROPPED	NUMBER SORTIES	TONS DROPPED	NUMBER† SORTIES
August	65,855	10,013 10,271	44,120	22,967	27,859	12,194	277	3,437
September	52,587	6,428 9,643	36,332	18,268	20,856	10,056	480	3,698
October	61,204	10,193 6,713	38,961	19,082	16,257	9,567	430	3,416
November	53,022	9,589 5,055	36,091	17,003	17,297	9,259	342	4,604
December	49,040	11,239 3,656	36,826	18,252	18,757	10,050	761	4,653
TOTAL	525,518	113,352 44,096	389,119	210,544	240,260	114,840	2,422	22,317
1945								
January	32,923	9,603 1,304	34,891	16,702	6,784	4,002	395	2,460
February	45,889	13,715 3,685	46,088	22,884	24,508	13,444	1,085	4,690
March	67,637	11,585 9,606	65,962	31,169	30,265	14,939	1,086	3,954
April	34,954	8,822 5,001	41,632	20,514	29,258	15,846	1,561	4,546
May	337	349 1,068	—	2,276	84	42	101	373
TOTAL	181,740	44,074 20,664	188,573	93,545	90,899	48,273	4,228	16,023
GRAND TOTAL	883,328	232,128 67,598	623,288	332,904	344,303	166,937	6,650	38,340

Table 24 Tons Bombs Dropped and Sorties Flown Against Japan by 20 US Air Force June 1944-August 1945‡

MONTH	NUMBER SORTIES FLOWN	TONS BOMBS DROPPED H.E.	INCENDIARY
1944 June		501	46
July		209	—
August		184	68
September		521	—
October		1,023	646
November		1,758	447
December		3,051	610
TOTAL	2,102	7,247	1,817

MONTH	NUMBER SORTIES FLOWN	TONS BOMBS DROPPED H.E.	INCENDIARY
1945 January		2,511	899
February		2,401	1,619
March		4,105	11,138
April		13,209	4,283
May		6,937	17,348
June		9,954	22,588
July		9,388	33,163
August		8,438	12,591
TOTAL	26,724	56,943	103,629
GRAND TOTAL	28,826	64,190	105,446

‡ 20 US Air Force was by far the most important formation attacking Japan proper. Other Air Forces achieved only the following modest tonnages against this target:

US Navy	6,788
7 US Air Force	5,102
5 US Air Force	1,905
13 US Air Force	6
TOTAL	13,801

Table 16 Tank strengths of Panzer Divisions in Normandy, on Dates Known, June-August 1944

DIVISION	21 Pz	12SS Pz	Pz Lehr	2 Pz	2SS Pz	1SS Pz	9SS Pz	10SS Pz	116 Pz
MONTH **June**	6th 127 7th 70	6th 177 7th 90	6th 182 25th 66	6th 161	1st 69	1st 88			
July	1st 40	1st 51 8th 85	7th 30 25th 45 26th 14		23rd 57	2nd 80			30th 62
August	23rd 10	7th 54 8th 48 10th 39 15th 15 23rd 10	5th 13 6th 9	7th 45 13th 25 19th 15 23rd 0	23rd 15	7th 60 13th 30 23rd 0	21st 25 23rd 22	23rd 0	7th 60 23rd 12

During June and July 1944, the Allies committed a little over 5,000 tanks in this theatre, and even that figure only includes tanks actually with the combat units.

PART III AIR FORCES

The air forces of the Second World War present a particular problem in a book of this nature. Except for production figures (see Section 7) and figures on strategic bombing (see the later tables in this section) the available figures are sporadic and imprecise such that it is rarely possible to compile detailed comparative tables. A particular problem is that even when figures are given they do not specify the category of aircraft involved e.g. combat or non-combat, first-line or second-line, full establishment or actually operational, serviceable or non-serviceable. Sadly, therefore, this section contains only a few comparative tables, presented first, and is perforce mainly taken up with a listing of available data country by country.

Comparative Strengths

Table 17 German and Allied Front-line Combat Aircraft At Selected Dates September 1939-April 1945

DATE	GERMANY	USA*	USSR†	UK	TOTAL ALLIED
September 1939	2,916	—	—	1,660	1,660
August 1940	3,015	—	—	2,913	2,913
December 1940	2,885	—	—	1,064 ‡	1,064
June 1941	3,451	—	8,105	3,106	11,211
December 1941	2,561	4,000 Δ 957	2,495	4,287	6,782**
June 1942	3,573	? 1,902	3,160	4,500††	9,562
December 1942	3,440	10,885 4,695	3,088	5,257	13,040 ‡‡
June 1943	5,003	? 8,586	8,290	6,026	22,902
December 1943	4,667	23,807 11,917	8,500	6,646	27,063 ‡‡
June 1944	4,637	? 19,342	11,800	8,339	39,481
December 1944	5,041	33,179 19,892	14,500	8,395	42,787 ‡‡
April 1945	2,175	31,335 21,572	17,000	8,000 ‡	46,752 ‡‡

* US Army Air Force only.
† Includes *Stavka* Reserve, which was apportioned among key army groups prior to a major offensive. At other times front-line strengths were some 25 per cent less e.g. Dec 43 5,775; June 44 8,798; Dec 44 11,530.
‡ Fighters only.

Δ In the USA column the top figure is total aircraft available, the bottom figure total aircraft overseas.
** Does not include USA.
†† Estimate.
‡‡ Includes US aircraft overseas only.

Table 45 Total US Marine Corps Squadrons at End of Year and Totals, by Type, Involved in Combat Operations, 1940-45

YEAR	Total Squadrons available by end of year	Total Combat Squadrons Starting Combat Operations				
		Fighter	Torpedo Bomber	Scout Bomber	Medium Bomber	Cumulative Total
1940	10	—	—	—	—	—
1941	13	1	2	—	—	3
1942	41	9	4	2	—	18
1943	88	12(1)‡	4	6	—	40
1944	145*	13(5)	2	4	6	65
1945	132†	11(1)	1	—	—	77
TOTAL	—	46(7)	13	12	6	77
NUMBER SAW NO COMBAT	?	20(1)	10	10	4	44

* Sept 30.

† Aug 31.

‡ Figure in brackets denotes number of total which were night-fighter squadrons.

Table 46 Sorties Flown in Pacific by US Forces 1941-45

YEAR	USAAF (excluding 20 US Air Force)	20 US Air Force	US Navy and Marine Air	TOTAL
1941/2	7,447	—	3,023	10,470
1943	102,092	—	16,132	118,224
1944	195,879	2,102	128,942	326,923
1945	170,365	26,724	110,012	307,101
TOTAL	475,783	28,826	258,109	762,718

USSR

Details on Red Air Force organisation are meagre and such figures as are available have already appeared in other Tables. Therefore, see Supplement to Table 2 for the growth of the Air Armies and Table 20 for aircraft strengths at certain dates. Table 93, listing aircraft production, gives some idea of the proportions of different types of aircraft.

YUGOSLAVIA

In March 1941, the paper front-line strength of the Yugoslav Air Force was 400 aircraft. Only 235 of these were in any sense modern i.e. 135 fighters (70 Bf 109E, 30 Hurricanes, 30 Hawker Furies, 5 Ikarus IK-2), 160 bombers (70 Dornier Do 171C, 40 Savoia Marchetti S.M. 79, 50 Blenheim I) and 40 reconnaissance (30 Breguet 19, 10 Caproni Ca 30). These were organised into 8 Air Regiments of 48 squadrons.

In 1944 two Yugoslav squadrons were formed within the RAF. Both flew fighters with the Balkan Air Force, 351 Squadron formed July and 352 formed April. There were also a fighter and a ground attack squadron fighting with the Red Air Force.

PART IV NAVIES

The first Table gives the naval strengths of all the belligerents at the beginning of the war. Though there is no Table giving comparative strengths for subsequent years, it should be noted that, for the major powers, these strengths can be deduced by combining the Table below with Tables 95 (Naval Production) and 65 (Naval Losses). The second Table in this section gives comparative naval strengths at all the major naval battles of the war. It combines exactly with Table 65 which lists comparative naval losses. The final Table gives some details on the strengths of the Commonwealth and government-in-exile navies throughout the war.

Table 47 Naval Strengths of the Belligerent Nations on Entry into the War

	AIRCRAFT CARRIERS	BATTLESHIPS	CRUISERS	DESTROYERS	ESCORTS	SUBMARINES
Australia	—	—	6	—	7	—
Brazil	—	2	2	13	—	4
Canada	—	—	—	6	—	—
China	—	—	6	—	?	—
Denmark	—	2*	1	—	—	12
Finland	—	2*	—	—	—	5
France	1	7	19	70	—	77
Germany	—	5	6	17†	—	57
Greece	—	—	2‡	10	—	6
India	—	—	—	—	5	—
Italy	—	2	22	59	—	115
Japan**	10	10	36	113	—	63
Netherlands	—	—	5	8	—	21
New Zealand††	—	—	2	—	—	—
Norway	—	—	—	8	—	5
Poland	—	—	—	4	—	5
Rumania	—	—	—	4	—	—
UK	8	12	50	94	87	38
USA**	8	17	36	171	—	112
USSR	—	2	2	47	—	75
Yugoslavia	—	—	1+1‡	3	—	4

* Coastal Defence.

† Serviceable.

‡ Antiquated.

** December 1941.

†† The Royal New Zealand Navy was created 1.10.41. Prior to that it was New Zealand Division, Royal Navy.

Table 48 Comparative Strengths in Major Naval Engagements 1939-45

Mediterranean and Atlantic

Δ Includes battlecruisers.

BATTLE AND DATE		SHIPS PRESENT				NOTES
		A/Cr.	B/s.Δ	Cr.	Dest.	
RIVER PLATE 13/12/39	British	—	—	3	—	
	Germans	—	1	—	—	
NARVIK 9-13/4/40	British	1	1	—	14	Total Fleets available during the whole period of the Norway Campaign were: British: 3 aircraft carriers; 7 battleships; 19 cruisers; c. 30 destroyers German: 3 battleships; 6 cruisers; 18 destroyers
	Germans	—	—	—	10	
NORWAY EVACUATION 4-9/6/40	British	2	—	3	10	
	Germans	—	2	1	4	
MERS EL-KEBIR 3/7/40	British	1	3	2	11	The French ships were in harbour.
	French	—	4	—	11	

Table 51 Military and Civilian Casualties of the Belligerent Nations 1939-45 (continued)

COUNTRY	POPULATION	No. SERVED IN FORCES	FORCES CASUALTIES				TOTAL CIVILIAN CASUALTIES
			KILLED & MISSING	WOUNDED	P.O.W.	TOTAL KILLED & WOUNDED	
S. AFRICA	10,000,000 (inc. 2.1 m. white)	250,000	8,700	14,400	14,600	23,100	–
UK	47,500,000	5,896,000	305,800	277,100	172,600	582,900	146,800 inc. 60,600 killed
USA	129,200,000	16,354,000	405,400	670,800	139,700	1,076,200	–
USSR	194,100,000	c. 30,000,000	11,000,000	?	c. 6,000,000	?	6,700,000
YUGOSLAVIA	15,400,000	?	Estimates of total Yugoslav deaths 1941-45 1.5 to 1.7 million.				

Table 52 Battle Casualties by Service of the Armed Forces of the Major Belligerents 1939-45

COUNTRY		No. SERVED	KILLED & MISSING	WOUNDED	P.O.W.
USA	Army *	c. 7,900,000 †	165,800	574,300	79,800
	Air Force *	c. 3,400,000	54,700	17,900	40,200
	Navy	4,183,000	36,900	37,800	?
	Marines	669,000	19,600	67,200	?
USSR‡		Forces breakdown not available			
UK	Army	3,778,000†	177,800	239,600	152,076
	Air Force Δ	1,185,000	76,300	22,800	13,100
	Navy ◊	923,000	51,600	14,700	7,400
GERMANY **	Army	c. 13,000,000	1,622,600	4,188,000	1,646,300††
	Air Force	c. 3,400,000	294,900‡‡	216,600‡‡	?
	Navy ΔΔ	c. 1,500,000	149,200	25,300	?
JAPAN ◊◊	Army	c. 6,300,000†	1,526,000	85,600	} 41,500
	Navy	c. 2,100,000	414,900	8,900	

* The Army Air Force was technically part of the US Army and it should be borne in mind that many sources lump their casualty figures together.

† Of these 4,950,000 US Army personnel served overseas and 2,640,000 British Army, and 2,100,000 Japanese Army. It is these troops who sustained the battle casualties.

‡ See Table 51 for the aggregate forces figure. The Red Army accounted for the vast proportion of these casualties. In December 1943, for example, the total strength of the Navy was only 266,000 men and the Air Force 483,000.

Δ Bomber Command's aircrew losses were 59,423 killed and missing out of 125,000 served, a mortality rate of 47.5 per cent.

◊ Not including the Merchant Navy, whose casualties were 34,902 killed and missing, 4,707 wounded and 5,720 p.o.w.

** To 31 January 1945 only.

†† The p.o.w. figure includes all missing, most of whom perished.

ΔΔ The Navy's U-Boat offensive involved 39,000 officers and men. Of these 32,000 were killed and missing (82 per cent) and 5,000 p.o.w.s.

‡‡ Most of these were members of the Luftwaffe Field Divisions. Aircrew losses (to 31/1/45) were 69,623 killed and missing, and 27,294 wounded.

◊◊ The Japanese Army and Navy each had their own air force.

PART II GROUND FORCES

Table 52 in the preceding subsection gives details on total army casualties for the major belligerents, and so the table below breaks these figures down by individual campaign. Figures for the lesser participants in these campaigns are also included and it should be remembered that many of these e.g., France 1940 (Belgians) or Eastern Front (Hungarians) represent the larger portion of a country's ground casualties throughout the war. The subsequent tables (54-60) present data relating to one or two countries only but are included because that data can be taken as fairly typical of the combat experience of most of the belligerents.

Table 53 Army Battle Casualties in Major Campaigns 1939-45

CAMPAIGN		BATTLE CASUALTIES		
		KILLED & MISSING	WOUNDED	P.O.W.
POLAND				
	Poles	66,300	133,700	787,000
	Germans	13,110	27,280	—
	Russians	900	?	?
DENMARK/NORWAY				
	Danes	—	—	—
	Norwegians	2,000	?	?
	Germans *	3,692	1,600	—
FRANCE 1940				
	Dutch	2,890	6,900	?
	Belgians	7,500	15,850	200,000
	French	120,000	250,000	1,450,000
	British †	11,010	14,070	41,340
	Germans	43,110	111,640	—
	Italians	1,250	4,780	—
BALKANS 1941				
	Yugoslavs	?	?	?
	Greeks •	19,000	70,000	?
	Germans Δ	3,674		—
	Italians #	38,830	50,870	—
EASTERN FRONT				
	Russians	c. 11,000,000	?	c. 6,000,000
	Germans ◊	2,415,690	3,498,060	?
	Italians	84,830	30,000	?
	Rumanians I‡	381,000	243,000	?
	Rumanians II‡	170,000		?
	Hungarians	136,000	c. 250,000	?
	Poles	at least 40,000		?
	Bulgarians	32,000		?

CAMPAIGN		BATTLE CASUALTIES		
		KILLED & MISSING	WOUNDED	P.O.W.
W. DESERT				
	British	c. 7,000	?	?
	Indians	1,720	3,740	9,790
	Australians	3,150	8,320	9,250
••	N. Zealanders	6,340	32,870	8,520
	S. Africans	2,100	3,930	14,250
	Germans	12,810	?	} 266,600 ††
	Italians	20,720	?	
TUNISIA				
	Americans	3,620	9,250	4,640
	British	6,230	21,260	10,600
	Indians	included in W. Desert		
	N. Zealanders	included in W. Desert		
	French	total military casualties= 12,920		
	Germans	included in W. Desert		
	Italians	included in W. Desert		
ITALY				
	Americans	29,560	82,180	7,410
	British	89,440		?
	Indians ‡‡	4,720	17,310	46
	Canadians	5,400	19,490	1,000
	N. Zealanders	included in W. Desert		
	Poles	2,460	8,640	?
	S. Africans	710	2,670	160
	French	8,660	23,510	?
	Brazilians	510	1,900	?
	Germans##	59,940	163,600	357,090

Table continues on following page

* Includes Navy and Air Force.

† Evacuated wounded only.

• Figure is for the whole war.

Δ German battle casualties in the Balkans up to 31 December 1944 were 34,040 killed and missing and 55,070 wounded.

Figures for Greece October 1940-April 1941. In April 1941 the Italians lost a further 3,330 killed and wounded in Yugoslavia, whilst anti-Partisan operations in that country, up to the Armistice of September 1943, cost another 30,360 men killed and wounded.

◊ From September 1939 to 31 December 1944. Prisoners-of-war are included in KILLED & MISSING. Figures include SS and foreign volunteers. Another set of figures, for the Field Army only, between 22 June 1941 and 10 March 1945, gives 1,001,680 killed, 1,287,140 missing and 3,968,260 wounded.

‡ I = fighting with Germans; II = fighting with Russians.

•• Includes casualties in Tunisia and Italy.

†† Prisoners-of-war in Tunisia only.

‡‡ To February 1945.

From September 1939 to 31 December 1944. German killed and missing is killed only. Figures include SS and foreign volunteers. Another set of figures, for the Field Army only, between June 1941 and 10 April 1945 gives 46,800 killed, 208,240 missing and 168,570 wounded.

Table 53 Army Battle Casualties in Major Campaigns 1939-45 (continued)

CAMPAIGN		BATTLE CASUALTIES		
		KILLED & MISSING	WOUNDED	P.O.W.
N.W.EUROPE				
	Americans	109,820	356,660	56,630
	British	30,280	96,670	14,700
	Canadians	10,740	30,910	2,250
	French	12,590	49,510	4,730
	Poles	1,160	3,840	370
	Germans ◊◊	128,030	399,860	7,614,790
PACIFIC ***				
	Americans	55,060	162,230	30,000
	Japanese	685,230	?	37,280
S.E.ASIA				
	British †††	5,670	12,840	53,230
	Indian	6,860	24,200	68,890
	African	860	3,210	200
	Australian	1,820	1,370	18,130
	American	3,650	2,600	680
	Japanese	210,830	?	3,100
CHINA				
	Chinese	Total Military casualties= 3,211,420		
	Japanese	388,600	?	1,060

◊◊ From September 1939 to 31 December 1944. KILLED & MISSING is killed only. The prisoner-of-war figures include 3,404,950 disarmed after the surrender and applies only to the Western Front. Figures include SS and foreign volunteers. Another set of figures, for the Field Army only, between June 1941 and 10 April 1945, gives 80,820 killed, 490,260 missing and 265,526 wounded.

*** These figures, it should be borne in mind, are for the Army (and Marines) only. The Japanese Navy lost a further 414,880 men killed whilst the major portion of the 36,950 US Navy men killed and 37,780 wounded in the war were serving in the Pacific.

††† Missing included in prisoners-of-war.

Casualty figures given thus far can be somewhat misleading in that they give a false impression of the lot of the *fighting* soldier in the Second World War. If data from Table 52, for example, were rendered into simple percentages of soldiers killed per number that served overall (even including only all those who served overseas) then it would seem that we were dealing with a much 'cheaper' conflict than, say, the First World War on the Western Front. And it is true that a soldier *just* inducted in 1941, for example, did stand, at that particular moment, a much greater chance of coming through the war unscathed than a predecessor in 1915. But, if he were unlucky enough to be posted to a rifle company, the men who did most of the actual fighting, then his chances of survival were not much better than an equivalent 'Tommy' or 'Doughboy'. The tables following show this fairly clearly, using casualty data on certain British and US infantry divisions that fought in N.W.Europe in 1944-45. Appalling though they are, these figures are not exceptionally severe. Only the Japanese in the Pacific and S.E.Asia, thanks to their disinclination to surrender, endured worse casualty rates and in no theatre of war were the rifleman's expectations much better.

Table 54 Battle Casualties of Selected US Infantry Divisions in North-West Europe 1944-45 and Percentage Riflemen who Became Casualties

DIVISION	MONTHS IN EUROPE	TOTAL CASUALTIES		PERCENTAGE†	
		DEAD	WOUNDED	DEAD	WOUNDED
4	11	4,834	17,371	18.1	65.1
29	11	3,786	15,541	15.9	56.3
30	11	3,516	13,376	16.5	62.7
79	11	2,943	10,971	16.1	59.8
83	11	3,620	11,807	19.2	62.5
90	11	3,930	14,386	17.3	63.2
5	10	2,656	9,549	15.9	60.3
8	10	2,820	10,057	16.3	60.8
35	10	2,947	11,526	15.6	61.0
28	9	2,683	9,609	16.1	57.7
80	9	3,480	12,484	17.0	61.0

† Percentage of a Division's riflemen (including replacements) who became casualties assuming 90% all casualties were amongst the riflemen and an 85% replacement rate.

Table 55 Percentage of Officer and Other Rank Casualties in Selected British Rifle Battalions in North-West Europe 1944-45

UNIT	% HIT		% KILLED	
	Officers	ORs	Officers	ORs
50 (Northumbrian) Division*	65.9	50.0	16.5	8.7
15 (Scottish) Division *	72.2	62.9	28.7	16.8
6 K.O.S.B.	67.5	62.5	17.5	8.9
1 Royal Norfolk	72.1	64.5	17.4	17.0
1 Dorsetshire	70.6	62.0	25.9	13.2

* The nine rifle battalions only.

The following two tables also offer only sample data, relating in these cases to the location on the body of battle wounds and to the percentages of wounds caused by different weapons.

Table 56 Percentage Distribution of Battle Wounds over Human Body in Various US, British and Soviet Samples from World War II.

TYPE OF DATA	Head, Face & Neck	Chest	Abdominal	Arms & Shoulders	Legs
Body Area	12	16	11	2	39
Total Hits (Bougainville sample)	21	13	8	23	35
Fatal Hits (Bougainville sample)	47	25	15	5	8
Major Wounds (Europe sample)	15	10	6	28	41
(British M.E. sample)	14	11	6	69	
(Soviet sample)	9	12	6	28	45

Table 57 Percentage of Battle Wounds to British Soldiers Caused by Different Weapons 1939-45

CAUSAL AGENT	% OF WOUNDS
Mortar, grenade, aerial bomb, shell	75
Bullet, anti-tank mine*	10
Landmine, booby trap	10
Blast, crush	2
Chemical	2
Other	1

* Many smaller samples from individual theatres give a significantly higher proportion of wounds from bullets. Two British divisional samples from N.W.Europe in 1944 give 25.2 and 31.5 per cent, an El Alamein (Oct 1942) corps sample gives 42.8 per cent and a US Bougainville/New Georgia/Burma sample gives 38.4 per cent.

Of course, the physically wounded are not the only battle casualties and a considerable problem in the Second World War, as it had been in the First, was that of combat fatigue/neurosis, the updated appellation for 'shell shock'. The table below gives some idea of its prevalence in relation to 'ordinary' battle casualties in the US, Canadian and British armies.

Table 58 US, British and Canadian Army Battle Casualties (Wounded and Psychoneurotic) in Selected Theatres and Years 1943-44. (Number of Hospital Admissions per 1000 Ration Strength)

THEATRE	WOUNDED	PSYCHONEUROTIC	RATIO
US (1944)			
All Overseas	87	42	2.0:1
N.W.Europe	135	52	2.6:1
Mediterranean	113	42	2.7:1
S.W.Pacific	32	47	0.7:1
Pacific Ocean	26	28	0.9:1
China/Burma/India	10	20	0.5:1
UK (All Troops)			
Middle East 1943	22	9	2.4:1
Mediterranean 1944	55	21	2.6:1
N.W.Europe 1944*	65	12	5.9:1
India/Burma 1944	47	6	8.8:1
Canadian Italy Nov 43-June 44	3,102†	940†	3.3:1

* Average quarterly admissions per 1000 ration strength.
† Canadian totals are gross figures.

The last two tables in this subsection give some British and American figures on the relative incidence of battle and non-battle casualties and on the diseases which were the main causes of the latter.

Table 59 Relative Incidence of US and British Army Battle and Non-battle Casualties in Selected Theatres 1942-45. (Average Annual Number of Hospital Admissions per 1000 Ration Strength)

THEATRE	WOUNDS	INJURY	DISEASE
US Total	27	90	666
Total Overseas	68	113	689
Europe	94	111	696
Pacific	39	122	785
UK Europe	119	85	545
India/Burma (British)	81*	49	1,118
India/Burma (All)	43*	45	873

* 1944 and 1945 only.

Table 62 **Bomber Command and 8 US Air Force Losses 1939-45**

DATE		BOMBER COMMAND		8 US AIR FORCE	
		Planes lost	As % No. Sorties	Planes lost	As % No. Sorties
1939	Sept	17	13.8	—	—
	Oct	4	12.5	—	—
	Nov	1	5.3	—	—
	Dec	19	11.9	—	—
1940	Jan	—	—	—	—
	Feb	3	5.2	—	—
	Mar	12	4.1	—	—
	April	41	6.2	—	—
	May	73	3.0	—	—
	June	65	2.0	—	—
	July	79	3.4	—	—
	Aug	81	3.1	—	—
	Sept	87	2.7	—	—
	Oct	60	2.5	—	—
	Nov	86	4.3	—	—
	Dec	62	4.3	—	—
1941	Jan	28	2.5	—	—
	Feb	52	3.0	—	—
	Mar	75	4.0	—	—
	April	98	3.3	—	—
	May	76	2.8	—	—
	June	116	3.1	—	—
	July	188	4.9	—	—
	Aug	206	5.4	—	—
	Sept	153	5.3	—	—
	Oct	126	4.8	—	—
	Nov	104	5.9	—	—
	Dec	51	3.3	—	—
1942	Jan	88	3.9	—	—
	Feb	33	2.3	—	—
	Mar	80	3.4	—	—
	April	143	3.6	—	—
	May	115	4.1	—	—
	June	201	4.0	—	—
	July	190	4.5	—	—
	Aug	152	5.8	—	—
	Sept	175	4.8	2	1.1
	Oct	103	4.0	10	3.5
	Nov	64	2.9	13	2.5

DATE		BOMBER COMMAND		8 US AIR FORCE	
		Planes lost	As % No. Sorties	Planes lost	As % No. Sorties
1942	Dec	88	4.5	17	4.8
1943	Jan	101	3.4	18	5.3
	Feb	107	2.0	23	4.4
	Mar	168	3.1	21	2.2
	April	265	4.5	29	6.5
	May	253	4.6	69	4.1
	June	275	4.7	90	4.3
	July	188	3.0	118	4.2
	Aug	275	3.5	117	5.2
	Sept	191	3.5	98	3.0
	Oct	159	3.4	186	6.6
	Nov	162	3.1	95	2.3
	Dec	170	4.1	172	2.9
1944	Jan	314	5.0	203	3.2
	Feb	199	4.6	271	2.7
	Mar	283	2.8	345	3.0
	April	214	2.2	420	2.9
	May	274	2.4	376	1.9
	June	305	1.9	320	1.1
	July	241	1.4	352	1.5
	Aug	221	1.1	331	1.4
	Sept	137	0.9	374	2.0
	Oct	127	0.8	177	0.9
	Nov	139	0.9	209	1.2
	Dec	119	0.8	119	0.6
1945	Jan	133	1.2	314	1.9
	Feb	173	1.0	196	0.9
	Mar	215	1.0	266	0.9
	April	73	0.5	190	0.9

Table 63 **15 US Air Force Bomber Losses 1943-45**

DATE		Planes lost	As % No. Sorties	DATE		Planes lost	As % No. Sorties
1943	Nov	28	1.6	**1944**	Aug	254	2.1
	Dec	36	1.8		Sept	94	0.9
1944	Jan	54	1.1		Oct	140	1.5
	Feb	128	3.2		Nov	132	1.4
	Mar	85	1.4		Dec	205	2.0
	April	194	1.9	**1945**	Jan	88	2.2
	May	175	1.2		Feb	147	1.1
	June	196	1.7		Mar	149	1.0
	July	317	2.5		April	83	0.5

Table 64 Incidence of Diseases, Psychoneurosis and Combat and Non-Combat Injuries Amongst RAF General Duties Officers and Aircrew 1939-45. (Annual Number Hospital Admissions per 1000 Ration Strength)

YEAR		ALL DISEASES	UPPER RESPIRATORY TRACT	ALIMENTARY	EAR, NOSE & THROAT	VENEREAL	PSYCHO-NEUROSIS	ALL INJURIES
1939	Gen. duties Officers	245	99	24	15	6	3	91
	Aircrew	142	55	10	5	8	1	64
1940	Gen. duties Officers	468	209	30	22	9	9	304
	Aircrew	342	153	19	12	7	4	188
1941	Gen. duties Officers	490	158	39	35	15	19	338
	Aircrew	255	97	15	12	7	7	144
1942	Gen. duties Officers	410	116	44	30	12	13	225
	Aircrew	389	135	37	13	11	6	146
1943	Gen. duties Officers	403	131	48	27	8	10	196
	Aircrew	492	203	46	16	12	7	165
1944	Gen. duties Officers	408	103	54	31	11	15	186
	Aircrew	540	181	56	19	18	9	159
1945	Gen. duties Officers	322	80	46	23	14	8	85
	Aircrew	349	88	45	15	23	9	86

PART IV NAVAL LOSSES

Some details on the personnel losses in the major navies of the Second World War will be found in Table 52, at the beginning of this section, and some figures on merchant navy crewmen lost are given in Tables 74 and 75 below. The main emphasis, however, is on ships lost and the manner of their sinking and it should be noted that additional figures on ship losses, by type and class, can be found in Table 100 in Section 8 on HARDWARE.

Table 65 Naval Losses of the Major Belligerents 1939-45

		AIRCRAFT CARRIERS	BATTLE-SHIPS	CRUISERS	DESTROYERS	ESCORT	SUBMARINES
USA	Total	11	2	10	71	10	53
	In Pacific	10	2	10	56	5	49
UK	Total	8	5	30*	110	58	77
	In Mediterranean	2	1	19	45	19	41
USSR		—	1	3	33	—	c. 100
AUSTRALIA		—	—	3	4	2	—
CANADA		—	—	—	6	11	—
JAPAN		19	8 Δ	37	134 ‡	—	130
GERMANY †		—	9 (3)	7 (3)	44 (6) ‡	—	785 (17)
ITALY		—	1	11	84 ‡	—	84

* Includes 3 cruiser-minelayers.

† Figures in brackets represent number scuttled. A further 221 U-Boats were scuttled after the surrender.

‡ Includes equivalents to destroyer escorts.

Δ Three other battleships which foundered in port are regarded by US statisticians as having been sunk in air attacks.

Table 91 Annual Allied and Axis Production of Military Trucks and Lorries 1939-45 (units)

DATE	USA	USSR	UK	TOTAL	GERMANY	ITALY	JAPAN	TOTAL
1939	} 32,604	?	?	?	32,558	?	?	?
1940		?	89,582	?	53,348	?	38,056	?
1941	183,614	?	88,161	?	51,085	?	46,389	?
1942	619,735	30,400	87,499	**737,634**	58,049	?	35,386	?
1943	621,502	45,600	113,912	**781,014**	74,181	?	c. 24,000	?
1944	596,963	52,600	54,615	**704,178**	67,375	?	20,356	?
1945	327,893	68,500	47,174	**443,567**	9,318	?	1,758	?
TOTAL	**2,382,311**	**197,100**	**480,943**	**3,060,354**	**345,914**	**83,000**	**165,945**	**594,859**

Table 92 Annual Allied and Axis Military Aircraft Production 1939-45 (units)

DATE	USA	USSR	UK	CANADA	EASTERN GROUP	TOTAL	GERMANY	ITALY	HUNGARY	RUMANIA	JAPAN	TOTAL
1939	5,856	10,382	7,940	?	?	**24,178**	8,295	1,692	—	?	4,467	**14,454**
1940	12,804	10,565	15,049	?	?	**38,418**	10,826	2,142	—	?	4,768	**17,736**
1941	26,277	15,735	20,094	?	?	**62,106**	11,776	3,503	—	?	5,088	**20,367**
1942	47,836	25,436	23,672	?	?	**96,944**	15,556	2,818	6	?	8,861	**27,235**
1943	85,898	34,845	26,263	?	?	**147,006**	25,527	967	267	?	16,693	**43,454**
1944	96,318	40,246	26,461	?	?	**163,025**	39,807	—	773	?	28,180	**68,760**
1945	49,761	20,052	12,070	?	?	**81,883**	7,544	—	?	—	8,263	**15,807**
TOTAL	**324,750**	**157,261**	**131,549**	**16,431**	**3,081**	**633,072**	**189,307**	**11,122**	**1,046**	**c.1,000**	**76,320**	**89,488**

Table 93 Annual Allied and Axis Military Aircraft Production, by Type 1939-45 (units)

FIGHTERS

DATE	USA	USSR	UK	TOTAL	GERMANY*	ITALY	JAPAN	TOTAL
1939	–	–	1,324	**1,324**	605	?	?	?
1940	1,162	4,574	4,283	**10,019**	2,746	1,155	?	?
1941	4,416	7,086	7,064	**18,566**	3,744	1,339	1,080	**6,163**
1942	10,769	9,924	9,849	**30,542**	5,515	1,488	2,935	**9,938**
1943	23,988	14,590	10,727	**49,305**	10,898	528	7,147	**18,573**
1944	38,873	17,913	10,730	**67,516**	26,326	—	13,811	**40,137**
1945	20,742	c. 9,000	5,445	**35,187**	5,883	—	5,474	**11,357**
TOTAL	**99,950**	**63,087**	**49,422**	**212,459**	**55,727**	**4,510**	**30,447**	**90,684**

* Includes jets:
1944= 1,041;
1945= 947.
Total= 1,988.

GROUND ATTACK

DATE	USA	USSR	UK	TOTAL	GERMANY	ITALY	JAPAN	TOTAL
1939	—	—	—	—	134	—	—	**134**
1940	—	—	—	—	603	—	—	**603**
1941	—	1,543	—	**1,543**	507	—	—	**507**
1942	—	8,219	—	**8,219**	1,249	—	—	**1,249**
1943	—	11,177	—	**11,177**	3,266	—	—	**3,266**
1944	—	11,110	—	**11,110**	5,496	—	—	**5,496**
1945	—	c. 5,500	—	**c. 5,500**	1,104	—	—	**1,104**
TOTAL	**—**	**37,549**	**—**	**37,549**	**12,539**	**—**	**—**	**12,539**

Fighters (continued)

TYPE	DATE IN SERVICE	SPEED (mph at feet.)	RANGE (miles)	CEILING (feet.)	RATE OF CLIMB (min/sec. to feet.)	ARMAMENT	NUMBER PRODUCED
NETHERLANDS 1940	Two types of fighter were available in May, the Fokker D.XXI and G.I.						
NEW ZEALAND	New Zealand squadrons fought both in Europe, under RAF command, and in the Pacific, under control of US South Pacific Command. Main types employed were Brewster Buffalos, Curtiss Kittyhawks, Chance Vought Corsairs (see USA below), Hawker Hurricanes, Supermarine Spitfires, Hawker Tempests and Typhoons (see UK below).						
NORWAY 1940	Only a few Gloster Gladiators were available when Germany attacked in April.						
POLAND							
P.Z.L. P-7a (bi-plane)	1932	200 at 13,100	350	27,100	1/38 to 3,300	2 x 7.7mm m.g.	153
P.Z.L. P-11c	pre-war	240 at 18,000	435	26,250	6/0 to 16,400	2 x 7.7mm m.g. max. bombs 110 lb.	330
RUMANIA	As well as German supplied Messerschmitt Bf 109E and Gs (see Germany above) and Heinkel He 112Bs, the Rumanians used the indigenously produced						
IAR 80A	1942	315 at 13,100	584	34,500	5/40 to 14,700	6 x 7.92mm m.g.	c. 180
SOUTH AFRICA	South African squadrons fought under Allied command in Africa and the Mediterranean, the most common fighters being the Curtiss Kittyhawk (see USA below) and the Supermarine Spitfire (see UK below).						
UNITED KINGDOM							
Bristol Beaufighter IF (night-fighter)	1940	306 at sea-level	1,500	28,900	1/0 to 1,850	4 x 20mm cannon 6 x 0.303in m.g.	5,920 / 1,150*
de Havilland Mosquito XIX (night-fighter)	1941 / 1944	380 at 13,200	1,000	33,000	1/0 to 2,700	4 x 20mm cannon	7,780† / 1,900*
de Havilland Mosquito Mk VI (fighter-bomber)	1941 / 1943	380 at 13,000	1,880	33,000	1/0 to 2,800	4 x 0.303in m.g. 4 x 20mm cannon max bombs 2,000 lb.	7,780† / 2,720
Gloster Meteor Mk III (jet)	1944	493 at 30,000	1,340	44,000	1/0 to 2,100 15/0 to 30,000	4 x 20mm cannon	316 (in war) / 280
Hawker Hurricane Mk I	1937	310 at 10,000	525	33,400	4/15 to 10,000	8 x 0.303in m.g.	14,230 / 3,900
Hawker Hurricane Mk IIC	1937 / 1940	330 at 18,000	920	35,600	1/0 to 2,700 12/30 to 30,000	4 x 20mm cannon max bombs 1,000 lb. or 8 x 3in rocket	14,230 / 6,650
Hawker Tempest Mk V (fighter-bomber)	1944	420 at 18,500	1,530	36,500	5/0 to 15,000	4 x 20mm cannon max bombs 2,000 lb. or 8 x 3in rocket	1,420 / 800
Supermarine Spitfire Mk IA	1938	360	395	31,900	1/0 to 2,500	8 x 0.303in m.g.	20,350 / 1,500
Supermarine Spitfire Mk VB	1938 / 1941	360 at 6,000	470	35,500	1/0 to 4,700	2 x 20mm cannon 4 x 0.303in m.g.	20,350 / 3,920
Supermarine Spitfire Mk IX	1938 / 1942	410 at 25,000	980	43,000	1/0 to 4,000	2 x 20mm cannon 4 x 0.303in m.g.	20,350 / 5,700
Supermarine Spitfire Mk XIV	1938 / 1944	440 at 24,500	850	43,000	1/0 to 4,600 7/0 to 20,000	2 x 20mm cannon 2 x 0.5in m.g.	20,350 / 960
USA							
Bell Airacobra P-39Q	1941 / 1943	385 at 11,000	675	35,000	4/50 to 15,000	1 x 37mm cannon 4 x 0.5in m.g. max bombs 500 lb.	9,590• / 4,900
Brewster Buffalo F2A-3	1939 / 1941	320 at 16,500	960	33,200	1/0 to 2,300	4 x 0.5in m.g.	510 / 200
Δ Curtiss Kittyhawk IA P-40E (fighter-bomber)	1939 / 1942	335 at 5,000	850	29,000	4/50 to 10,000	6 x 0.5in m.g. max bombs 500 lb.	13,740 / 2,320

* All night-fighter variants (inc. Beaufighter IIF and Mosquito II, XII, XIII, XV, XVIII and Mk 30).

† See also Mosquito under Bombers (UK).

• Over half the total production went to the USSR.

Δ In the USA, the P-40 was known as the Warhawk.

Fighters (continued)

TYPE	DATE IN SERVICE	SPEED (mph at feet.)	RANGE (miles)	CEILING (feet.)	RATE OF CLIMB (min/sec. to feet.)	ARMAMENT	NUMBER PRODUCED	
USA								
* Curtiss Kittyhawk IV P-40N-20 (fighter-bomber)	1939 / 1944	350 at 16,400	750	31,000	7/20 to 14,000	6 x 0.5in m.g. max bombs 1,500 lb.	13,740 / 5,200 x 'N'	* In the USA, the P-40 was known as the Warhawk.
Grumman Wildcat F4F-4 and FM-1 (carrier-fighter)	1940 / 1941	320 at 19,400	770	34,900	1/0 to 2,000	6 x 0.5in m.g. max bombs 200 lb.	7,350 / 2,310	
Grumman Hellcat F6F-5 (carrier-fighter)	1943 / 1944	380 at 23,400	950	37,300	1/0 to 3,000	6 x 0.5in m.g. or 2 x 20mm cannon + 4 x 0.5in m.g. max bombs 2,000 lb.	12,270 / 6,436	
Lockheed Lightning P-38G	1941 / 1942	345 at 5,000	1,400	39,000	1/50 to 5,000	1 x 20mm cannon 4 x 0.5in m.g. max bombs 2,000 lb.	9,390 / 1,080	
Lockheed Lightning P-38L	1941 / 1943	410 at 25,000	2,250	44,000	2/0 to 5,000	1 x 20mm cannon 4 x 0.5in m.g. max bombs 3,200 lb.	9,390 / 3,920	
North American Mustang P-51B/C	1942 / 1943	440 at 30,000	2,200	42,000	12/30 to 30,000	4 x 0.5in m.g. max bombs 2,000 lb.	15,470 / 3,750	
North American Mustang P-51D	1942 / 1944	440 at 25,000	2,100	41,900	13/1 to 30,000	6 x 0.5in m.g. max bombs 2,000 lb.	15,470 / 7,970	
Northrop Black Widow P-61A/B (night-fighter)	1944	360 at 20,000	3,000	33,100	12/0 to 20,000	4 x 20mm cannon 4 x 0.5in m.g. max bombs 6,400 lb.	740 / 650	
Republic Thunderbolt P-47D	1942 / 1943	430 at 30,000	590	42,000	11/0 to 20,000	6 or 8 x 0.5in m.g. max bombs 2,500 lb.	15,630 / 12,560	
Vought Corsair F4U-1 (carrier-fighter)	1943	415 at 20,000	1,015	37,000	1/0 to 3,100	6 x 0.5in m.g.	12,570 / 9,440†	† Including F4U-1, F3A-1, FG-1, FG-1D.
USSR								
Lavochkin La-5FN	1941 / 1943	400 at 6,400	475	31,100	4/42 to 16,400	2 x 20mm cannon or 1 x 23mm cannon	9,920 / ?	
Lavochkin La-7	1941 / 1944	410	395	34,450	4/30 to 16,400	2 or 3 x 20mm cannon max bombs 440 lb.	5,750	
Yakovlev Yak-1	1940	360 at 16,400	530	32,810	4/30 to 16,400	1 x 20mm cannon 2 x 7.6mm m.g. max bombs 440 lb. or 6 x 82mm rocket	8,700	
Yakovlev Yak-3	1943	405 at 3,300	560	35,430	4/6 to 16,400	1 x 20mm cannon 2 x 7.6mm m.g.	4,850	
Yakovlev Yak-7	1942	340 at sea-level	510	33,460	4/55 to 16,400	1 x 20mm cannon 1 x 12.7mm m.g. max bombs 440 lb. or 6 x 82mm rocket	6,400	
Yakovlev Yak-9D	1942	370 at 6,550	875	34,770	5/40 to 16,400	1 x 20mm cannon 1 x 12.7mm m.g.	16,800	

Dive and Torpedo Bombers and Ground Attack

TYPE	DATE IN SERVICE	SPEED (mph at feet.)	RANGE (miles)	CEILING (feet.)	RATE OF CLIMB (min/sec. to feet.)	ARMAMENT	NUMBER PRODUCED
GERMANY							
Focke-Wulf FW 190F-3 (ground-attack)	1941 / 1942	370 at 18,000	330	?	1/0 to 2,100	2 x 20mm cannon 2 x 7.9mm m.g. max bombs 550 lb.	20,000 / c. 500
Henschel Hs 129B-2 (ground-attack)	1942 / 1943	250 at 12,600	430	29,500	1/0 to 1,600	Variety of 20mm (2), 30mm (1), 37mm (1) cannon and 7.9mm (2) m.g. max bombs 770 lb.	870 / c. 450
Junkers Ju 87B-1/2 (dive-bomber)	1937 / 1938	240 at 13,400	490	26,150	4/20 to 6,600	3 x 7.9mm m.g. max bombs 1,100 lb.	5,710 / c. 1,350
Junkers Ju 87D-1 (dive-bomber)	1937 / 1941	255 at 13,500	950	23,900	19/50 to 16,400	3 x 7.9mm m.g. max bombs 4,000 lb.	5,710 / c. 3,300 x 'D'
JAPAN							
Aichi D3A2 'Val' (dive-bomber)	1937 / 1942	240 at 9,800	915	30,000	6/30 to 9,800	3 x 7.7mm m.g. max bombs 810 lb.	1,500 / 1,020
Nakajima B5N2 'Kate' (torpedo-bomber)	1938 / 1941	230 at 11,800	1,240	27,000	7/40 to 9,800	1 x 7.7mm m.g. max bombs 1,800 lb. or 1 x torpedo	1,150 / ?
Nakajima B6N2 'Jill' (torpedo-bomber)	1942 / 1944	300 at 16,000	1,900	29,700	10/25 to 16,400	2 x 7.7mm m.g. max bombs 1,800 lb. or 1 x torpedo	1,270 / 1,130
Yokosuka D4Y1 'Judy' (dive-bomber)	1942 / 1943*	340 at 15,600	980	32,500	5/15 to 9,900	2 x 7.7mm m.g. 1 x 7.92mm m.g. max bombs 680 lb.	2,040 / c. 800
UNITED KINGDOM							
Bristol Beaufourt Mk I (torpedo-bomber)	1940	265 at 6,000	1,600	16,500	?	6 x 0.303in m.g. max bombs 1,500 lb. max torpedo 1,600 lb.	1,130 / 960
Bristol Beaufighter Mk X (anti-shipping fighter)	1940 / 1942	300 at 13,000	1,470	15,000	3/30 to 5,000	4 x 20mm cannon 1 x 0.303in m.g. max bombs 1,650 lb. max torpedo 2,130 lb. or 8 x 90lb. rocket	5,920 / 2,100
Fairey Swordfish Mk I (torpedo-bomber)	1936	140 at 4,700	1,000	10,700	10/0 to 5,000	2 x 0.303in m.g. max bombs 1,500 lb. or 1 x 18" torpedo	2,390 / 990
Fairey Barracuda Mk II (torpedo/dive-bomber)	1942	230 at 1,700	1,150	16,600	6/0 to 5,000	2 x 0.303in m.g. max bombs 1,000 lb. or 1 x 1,620lb. torpedo	2,600 / 1,400
Hawker Typhoon IB (ground-attack)	1941	410 at 19,000	510	35,200	5/50 to 15,000	4 x 20mm cannon max bombs 2,000 lb. or 8 x 3" rocket	3,270 / c. 2,700
USA							
Curtiss Helldiver SB2C-4 (scout-bomber)	1943 / 1944	270 at sea-level	1,240	29,100	1/0 to 1,800	2 x 20mm cannon 2 x 0.3in m.g. max bombs 2,000 lb.	7,200 / 2,040
Douglas Dauntless SBD-5/A24-B (dive-bomber)	1940 / 1943	240 at 15,800	1,100	24,300	1/0 to 1,200	2 x 0.5in m.g. 2 x 0.3in m.g. max bombs 2,250 lb.	5,940 / 3,640
Grumman Avenger TBF-1/TBM-1 (torpedo-bomber)	1942	250 at sea-level	1,210	22,400	1/0 to 1,400	1 x 0.5in m.g. 2 x 0.3in m.g. max torpedo 1,600 lb.	9,800 / 5,170
Vultee Vengeance A-35B (dive-bomber)	1942 / 1943	280 at 13,500	2,300	22,300	11/20 to 15,000	7 x 0.5in m.g. max bombs 2,000 lb.	1,930 / 830

* qua dive-bomber. Originally reconnaissance aircraft

Bombers (continued)

TYPE	DATE IN SERVICE	SPEED (mph at feet.)	RANGE (miles)	CEILING (feet.)	RATE OF CLIMB (min/sec. to feet.)	ARMAMENT	NUMBER PRODUCED
JAPAN							
Kawasaki Ki-48-II 'Lily' (light x 2)*	1940 / 1942	310 at 18,400	1,500	33,100	8/30 to 16,400	3 x 7.7mm m.g. max bombs 1,750 lb.	1,120 / 410
Mitsubishi G3M2 'Nell' (medium x 2)	1937	230 at 13,700	2,700	30,000	8/20 to 9,800	1 x 20mm cannon 4 x 7.7mm m.g. max bombs 1,760 lb.	1,050 / c. 700
Mitsubishi Ki-21-IIa/b 'Sally' (heavy x 2)	1938 / 1941	300 at 15,500	1,700	32,800	13/15 to 19,600	1 x 12.7mm m.g. 5 x 7.7mm m.g. max bombs 2,200 lb.	2,060 / 1,280
Mitsubishi G4M1-11 'Betty' (medium x 2)	1941	270 at 13,800	3,750	28,000	18/0 to 23,000	1 x 20mm cannon 4 x 7.7mm m.g. max bombs 1,750 lb.	2,450 / 1,200
Mitsubishi G4M2-22 'Betty' (medium x 2)	1941 / 1943	270 at 15,000	3,270	29,300	30/20 to 26,000	2 x 20mm cannon 6 x 7.7mm m.g. max bombs 2,200 lb.	2,450 / 1,140 x M2 and M2a
Nakajima Ki-49-IIa/b 'Helen' (heavy x 2)	1938 / ?	300 at 16,400	1,830	30,500	13/40 to 16,400	1 x 20mm cannon 5 x 7.7mm m.g. max bombs 2,500 lb.	815 / 665
Yokosuka P1Y1 'Frances' (medium x 2)	1945	340 at 19,300	3,340	30,800	4/15 to 9,800	2 x 20mm cannon max bombs 2,200 lb.	1,100
POLAND 1939							
P.Z.L. P-23-B (light x 1)	1936	185 at 6,560	780	24,000	4/40 to 6,500	3 x 7.7mm m.g. max bombs 1,540 lb.	310
P.Z.L. P-37-B (medium x 2)	1938	280 at 11,100	2,800	30,300	?	3 x 7.7mm m.g. max bombs 5,700 lb.	95
UNITED KINGDOM							
Armstrong Whitworth Whitley Mk V (heavy x 2)	1937 / 1939	230 at 16,400	1,500	26,000	16/0 to 15,000	5 x 0.303in m.g. max bombs 7,000 lb.	1,810 / 1,470
Avro Lancaster I (heavy x 4)	1942	240 at sea-level	2,530	22,000	41/0 to 20,000	8 x 0.303in m.g. max bombs 18,000lb.	7,400 / 3,440
Bristol Blenheim IV (medium x 2)	1937 / 1939	260 at 12,000	1,460	22,000	1/0 to 1,500	2 or 4 x 0.303in m.g. max bombs 1,000 lb.	6,360 / 3,300
de Havilland Mosquito B. Mk XVI (light x 2)	1941 / 1942	410 at 26,000	1,480	37,000	1/0 to 2,800	max bombs 4,000 lb.	7,780† / 1,200
Fairey Battle Mk III (light x 1)	1937	260 at 15,000	1,000	25,000	4/0 to 5,000	2 x 0.303in m.g. max bombs 1,000 lb.	2,200 / ?
Handley Page Halifax B. Mk III (heavy x 4)	1940 / 1941	280 at 13,500	1,980	24,000	1/0 to 960	10 x 0.303in m.g. max bombs 13,000lb.	6,180 / 2,090
Handley Page Hampden Mk I (medium x 2)	1938	260 at 16,500	1,990	22,700	19/0 to 15,000	6 x 0.303in m.g. max bombs 4,000lb.	1,530 / 1,410
Short Stirling III (heavy x 4)	1940 / 1941	270 at 14,500	2,000	17,000	?	8 x 0.303in m.g. max bombs 14,000lb.	2,370 / 880
Vickers Wellington IC (medium x 2)	1938	230 at 15,500	2,550	18,000	1/0 to 1,120	6 x 0.303in m.g. max bombs 4,500lb.	11,460• / 2,680
USA							
Boeing Flying Fortress B-17F (heavy x 4)	1940 / 1942	325 at 25,000	3,800	35,000	25/40 to 20,000	12 x 0.5in m.g. 1 x 0.3in m.g. max bombs 17,600lb.	12,700 / 3,400

* 'x 2' indicates number of engines.

† Of which c. 2,100 were bombers. See also Fighters (UK).

• Including 2,320 for Coastal Command.

Bombers (continued)

TYPE	DATE IN SERVICE	SPEED (mph at feet.)	RANGE (miles)	CEILING (feet.)	RATE OF CLIMB (min/sec. to feet.)	ARMAMENT	NUMBER PRODUCED	
USA continued								
Boeing Flying Fortress B-17G (heavy x 4)*	1940 / 1943	300 at 25,000	3,400	35,600	37/0 to 20,000	13 x 0.5in m.g. max bombs 17,600 lb.	12,700 / 6,300	* 'x 4' indicates number of engines.
Boeing Superfortress B-29 (heavy x 4)	1944	360 at 25,000	5,600	31,800	38/0 to 20,000	10 x 0.5in m.g. max bombs 20,000 lb.	3,900 / 2,460	
Consolidated Liberator B-24D (heavy x 4)	1942	300 at 25,000	2,850	32,000	22/0 to 20,000	10 x 0.5in m.g. max bombs 8,800 lb.	18,500 / 2,750	
Consolidated Liberator B-24J (heavy x 4)	1942 / 1943	300 at 30,000	2,100	28,000	25/0 to 20,000	10 x 0.5in m.g. max bombs 8,800 lb.	18,500 / 7,700	
Douglas Havoc A-20G (light x 2)	1941 / 1943	340 at 12,400	1,100	25,800	7/5 to 10,000	10 x 0.5in m.g. max bombs 4,000 lb.	7,480† / 2,850	† Many went to USSR and RAF (where known as Bostons).
Douglas Invader A-26B (light x 2)	1944	350 at 15,000	1,800	31,300	8/5 to 10,000	10 or 18 x 0.5in m.g. max bombs 6,000 lb.	2,450 / 1,350	
Lockheed Hudson A-29/IIIA ● (light x 2)	1939 / 1940	250 at 15,000	2,800	26,500	6/20 to 10,000	5 x 0.3in m.g. max bombs 1,600 lb.	2,930 / c. 800	● Mainly flown by RAF Coastal Command.
Martin Marauder B-26B (medium x 2)	1941 / 1942	320 at 14,500	1,150	23,500	12/0 to 15,000	6 x 0.5in m.g. max bombs 5,200 lb.	4,700 / 1,880	
North American Mitchell B-25J (medium x 2)	1941 / 1943	275 at 13,000	2,700	23,800	19/0 to 15,000	14 x 0.5in m.g. max bombs 3,200 lb.	9,820 / 4,320	
USSR								
Ilyushin Il-4 DB-3F (medium x 2)	1938 / 1940	270 at 22,000	2,350	31,800	12/0 to 22,000	4 x 7.62mm m.g. max bombs 5,500 lb.	6,800 / 5,260	
Tupolev Tu-2S (medium x 2)	1944	340 at 17,700	1,240	31,200	9/30 to 16,400	2 x 20mm cannon 3 x 12.7mm m.g. max bombs 6,600 lb.	c. 1,000 (pre-VJ Day)	

Medals & Special Insignia

GOOD CONDUCT MEDAL
(Army)

Got Yours?

MEDAL OF HONOR
With Service Ribbon
(Army)
For conspicuous gallantry and intrepidity at the risk of life, above and beyond the call of duty, in action involving actual conflict with an opposing armed force.

MEDAL OF HONOR
With Service Ribbon
(Navy-Marine Corps-Coast Guard)
For conspicuous gallantry and intrepidity at the risk of life, above and beyond the call of duty, in action involving actual conflict with an opposing armed force.

**DISTINGUISHED
SERVICE CROSS**
(Army)
For extraordinary heroism in connection with military operations against an opposing armed force.

MEDAL OF HONOR
With Service Ribbon
(Air Force)
For conspicuous gallantry and intrepidity at the risk of life, above and beyond the call of duty, in action involving actual conflict with an opposing armed force.

NAVY CROSS
(Navy-Marine Corps-Coast Guard)
For extraordinary heroism in connection with military operations against an opposing armed force.

AIR FORCE CROSS

For extraordinary heroism in connection with military operations against an opposing armed force.

DISTINGUISED SERVICE MEDAL

For award by the Decretary of Defense for exceptionally meritorious service in a duty of great responsibility.

DISTINGUISED SERVICE MEDAL (Army)

For exceptionally meritorious service to the Government in a duty of great responsibility.

DISTINGUISED SERVICE MEDAL (Navy-Marine Corps)

For exceptionally meritorious service to the Government in a duty of great responsibility.

DISTINGUISED SERVICE MEDAL (Air Force)

For exceptionally meritorious service to the Government in a duty of great responsibility.

SILVER STAR

For gallantry in action against an opposing armed force.

LEGION OF MERIT

For exceptionally meritorious conduct in the performance of outstanding services.

DISTINGUISHED SERVICE CROSS

For heroism or extraordinary achievement while partipating in aerial flight. Bronze "V" device is worn by Navy Marine Corps personnel to denote valor.

SOLDIER'S MEDAL (Army)

For heroism that involves the voluntary risk of life under conditions other than those of conflict with an opposing armed force.

BRONZE STAR MEDAL

For heroic or meritorious achievement of service, not involving aerial flight, in connection with operations against an opposing armed force. Bronze "V" device worn to denote valor.

AIR MEDAL

For meritorious achievement while participating in aerial flight. Bronze "V" device worn to denote valor (Army-Navy-MarinE Corps)

GOOD CONDUCT MEDAL (Army)

Awarded for exemplary behavior, efficiency, and fidelity while on active duty. A clasp with loops denotes subsequent awards.

**GOOD CONDUCT MEDAL
(Navy)**
Based on conduct for four-year periods of continuous active service. Bronze stars denote subsequent awards.

**GOOD CONDUCT MEDAL
(Marine Corps)**
Based on conduct for three-year periods of continuous active service. Bronze stars denote subsequent awards.

**GOOD CONDUCT MEDAL
(Air Force)**
Awarded for exemplary behavior, efficiency, and fidelity. Oak leaf clusters denote subsequent awards.

**GOOD CONDUCT MEDAL
(Coast Guard**
Based on conduct for three-year periods (after 1 January 1980) of continuous active service. Bronze stars denote subsequent awards.

PURPLE HEART
Awarded for wounds or death as a result of an act of any opposing armed force.

**EUROPEAN-AFRICAN-MIDDLE
EASTERN CAMPAIGN MEDAL**
For service in the European-African-Middle Eastern Theater during World War II.

WORLD WAR II VICTORY MEDAL
For service in World War II.

United States Army - World War II
Army Groups

FIRST ARMY GROUP

SIXTH ARMY GROUP

TWELFTH ARMY GROUP

FIFTEENTH ARMY GROUP

Armies

1st Army

2nd Army

3rd Army

4th Army

5th Army

1st Army

7th Army

8th Army

9th Army

10th Army

15th Army

Army Air Forces

Army Air Forces

Mediterranean Allied Air Force

U.S. Strategic Air Force

1st Air Force

2nd Air Force

3rd Air Force

4th Air Force

5th Air Force

6th Air Force

7th Air Force

8th Air Force

9th Air Force

10th Air Force

11th Air Force

12th Air Force

13th Air Force

 14th Air Force

 15th Air Force

 20th Air Force

Defense & Base Commands

 Atlantic Base Commands

 Eastern Defense Command

 AA ARTY Command Western Defense Command

 AA ARTY Command Eastern Defense Command

 Iceland Base Command

 Greenland Base Command

 Bermuda Base Command

 Labrador, NE Canada Base Command

 Caribbean Defense Command

Theaters

 Supreme HQ Allied Expeditionary Force

 European Theater of Operations

 U.S. Army Forces - South Atlantic

 Headquarters SE Asia Command

 China-Burma-India Theater

 U.S. Army Forces - Pacific Ocean Area

 U.S. Army Forces - Middle East

 North African Theater of Operations

Army Ground Forces

Army Ground Forces

Armored Center

Replacement & School Command

AGF Replacement Depots

Antiaircraft Command

Airborne Command

Army Service Forces

Army Service Forces

Ports of Embarkation

1st Service Command

2nd Service Command

3rd Service Command

4th Service Command

5th Service Command

6th Service Command

7th Service Command

8th Service Command

9th Service Command

Northwest Service Command

Military District of Washington

ASF Training Center Units

Army Specialized Training Program

Army Specialized Training Program - Reserve

Infantry, Airborne, & Cavalry Divisions

 1st Div.

 2nd Div.

 3rd Div.

 4th Div.

 5th Div.

 6th Div.

 7th Div.

 8th Div.

 9th Div.

 10th Div.

 11th Div.

 13th Div.

 17th Div.

 24th Div.

 25th Div.

 26th Div.

 27th Div.

 28th Div.

 29th Div.

 30th Div.

 31st Div.

 32nd Div.

 33rd Div.

 34th Div.

 35th Div.

 36th Div.

 37th Div.

 38th Div.

 40th Div.

 41st Div.

 42nd Div.

 43rd Div.

 44th Div.

 45th Div.

 63rd Div.

 65th Div.

 66th Div.

 69th Div.

 70th Div.

 71st Div.

 75th Div.

 76st Div.

 77th Div.

 78th Div.

 79th Div.

 80th Div.

 81st Div.

 82nd ABN Div.

 83rd Div.

 84th Div.

 85th Div.

 86th Div.

 87th Div.

 88th Div.

 89th Div.

 90th Div.

 91st Div.

 92nd Div.

 93rd Div.

 94th Div.

 95th Div.

 96th Div.

 97th Div.

 98th Div.

 99th Div.

 100th Div.

  101st ABN Div.

 102nd Div.

 103rd Div.

 104th Div.

1st Cav. Div.

 106th Div.

Americal Division

 2nd Cav. Div.

Armored Divisions

1st Armored Division

2nd Armored Division

3rd Armored Division

4th Armored Division

5th Armored Division

6th Armored Division

7th Armored Division

8th Armored Division

9th Armored Division

10th Armored Division

11th Armored Division

12th Armored Division

13th Armored Division

14th Armored Division

Corps

I Corps

II Corps

III Corps

IV Corps

V Corps

VI Corps

VII Corps

VIII Corps

IX Corps

X Corps

XI Corps

XII Corps

XIII Corps · XIV Corps · XV Corps · XVI Corps

XVIII Corps · XIX Corps · XX Corps · XXI Corps

XXII Corps · XXIII Corps · XXIV Corps · XXVI Corps

Army Air Forces

2nd Bombardment · 2nd Troop Carrier · 4th Anti-Submarine · 4th Bombardment · 4th Combat Cargo

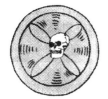   

6th Fighter · 7th Bombardment · 7th Fighter · 9th Bombardment · 9th Fighter

11th Bombardment · 11th Ferrying · 13th Bombardment · 15th Bombardment Light · 16th Photographic

| 16th Reconnaissance | 17th Pursuit | 19th Bombardment | 21st Tactical Reconnaissance | 24th Troop Carrier |

| 25th Bombardment | 26th Bombardment | 30th Bombardment | 30th Fighter | 31st Photographic Reconnaissance |

| 31st Bombardment | 34th Bombardment | 38th Fighter | 39th Fighter | 48th Bombardment |

| 48th Bombardment | 44th Fighter | 51st Fighter | 53rd Bombardment | 53rd Fighter |

| 59th Fighter | 61st Fighter | 72nd Bombardment | 72nd Liaison | 77th Fighter |

| 87th Bombardment | 90th Bombardment | 90th Fighter | 92nd Fighter | 94th Fighter |

95th Bombardment

96th Bombardment

96th Fighter

98th Bombardment

99th Fighter

316th Bombardment

316th Fighter

330th Fighter

331st Bombardment

334th Fighter

377th Bombardment

383rd Fighter

394th Bombardment

402nd Bombardment

408th Bombardment

413th Bombardment

424th Bombardment

429th Bombardment

434th Bombardment

434th Fighter

436th Bombardment

462nd Fighter

487th Fighter

499th Bombardment

502nd Bombardment

508th Fighter

509th Bombardment

512th Bombardment

513th Bombardment

526th Bombardment

531st Bombardment **532nd Bombardment** **552nd Bombardment** **554th Bombardment** **570th Bombardment**

575th Bombardment **584th Bombardment** **586th Bombardment** **587th Bombardment** **598th Bombardment**

600th Bombardment **644th Bombardment** **650th Bombardment** **668th Bombardment** **700th Bombardment**

753rd Bombardment **759th Bombardment** **772nd Bombardment** **774th Bombardment** **816th Bombardment**

819th Bombardment **820th Bombardment** **827th Bombardment** **840th Bombardment** **863rd Bombardment**

This poem was written by Kelly Strong in the spring of 1981 while he was attending Homestead High School in Homestead, Fl. As part of an assignment for his Air Force Junior ROTC class, he was asked to write a poem or story with the theme "Freedom Is Not Free." The Air Force Sergeants Association read it at their national convention in Fort Lauderdale that next year. Since then, Kelly has received letters and phone calls from people all over the country who read the poem and were touched in some way by its words.

Kelly Strong is currently a Lieutenant Commander in the Coast Guard living in Mobile, Al., where he is a flight instructor in the Falcon Jet. He and his wife, Najwa, have one son, Benjamin.

No, Freedom is Not Free

I watched the flag pass one day
It fluttered in the breeze.
A young Marine saluted it,
And then, he stood at ease.

I looked at him in uniform,
So young, so tall, so proud;
With hair cut square and eyes alert,
He'd stand out in any crowd,

I thought how many men like him
Had fallen through the years
How many died on foreign soil?
How many mother's tears?

How many pilot's planes shot down?
How many died at sea?
How many foxholes—soldiers graves?
No, freedom is not free.

I heard the sound of Taps one night,
When everything was still.
I listened to the bugler play
And felt a sudden chill.

I wondered just how many times
That Taps had meant "Amen"
When a flag had covered a casket
of a brother or a friend.

I thought of all the children,
Of the mothers and the wives,
Of fathers, sons, and husbands,
With interrupted lives.

I thought about the graveyard,
At the bottom of the sea,
Of unmarked graves in Arlington,
No, Freedom is Not Free!

by Kelly Strong

Conclusion

After two years, this effort has finally been completed. I wish to thank so many of you veterans who wrote or called wishing me success, and contributed songs, slang, war stories and cartoons to be included as part of this documentary.

I apologize for not including all your letters, but because of space limitations, repetitions, or length of material it was not practical. If more material is received as a result of this effort, I may consider a second edition.

What a wonderful experience to finally share this in book form, so we can all relive some of the nostalgia and memories of a time long ago.

I hope this book will eventually be a point of reference for our children and future generations, to paint a more descriptive picture of the life and times we shared and lived.

While researching and compiling all the material for this book, I was most interested in the quantity and diversity of songs that were so dominant during those years. The war years sparked a genius and creativity that probably will never be repeated in popular music.

I tried to represent all service branches and hope no one takes offense for not being represented equally. The material was determined by your responses.

Yes, we all shared a common bond. May this book be a stimulus for those of us who still treasure the memory of our friendships, our youthful enthusiasm and dedication to country.

I would be most appreciative to hear from you, with suggestions or comments.

Leonard Zerlin